DATE DUE

AP 16'02			
DE 17 05			
DE 04 08			
AP 3 09			

DEMCO 38-296

C. S. Lewis's
Case for the Christian Faith

C. S. Lewis's Case for the Christian Faith

Richard L. Purtill

1817

Harper & Row, Publishers, San Francisco

Cambridge, Hagerstown, New York, Philadelphia
London, Mexico City, São Paulo, Sydney

Library of Congress Cataloging in Publication Data

Purtill, Richard L.
   C. S. LEWIS'S CASE FOR THE CHRISTIAN FAITH.

   Bibliography: p. 141
   Includes index.
   1. Apologetics—History—20th century. 2. Lewis,
C. S. (Clive Staples), 1898–1963. I. Title.
BT1117.P87 1981   230'.092'4   81-47435
ISBN 0-06-066711-7   AACR2

81 82 83 84 85 10 9 8 7 6 5 4 3 2 1

This book is dedicated to
my friends and fellow Lewis enthusiasts

Ruth Cantor
Evan Gibson
Tom Howard
Clyde Kilby
Janet Knedlick
Mike Macdonald
Chad Walsh

Contents

Preface

This book aims to present, in a clear and understandable form, the main lines of C. S. Lewis's defense of and arguments for Christian belief and practice. Those who have read some of Lewis's writing will find familiar ideas, but perhaps also some new ones. Those—and there are many—who have read all of Lewis's writings will, I hope, find that this compendium of Lewis's thinking on many topics will help them to see him as a whole.

Some who read this book may be entirely unfamiliar with Lewis, or, for that matter, with Christianity; I hope that this book will make them want to know more about both. As most of my readers will probably have read at least some of Lewis's more popular works, where possible I have avoided the best-known works when quoting and made use of material from unpublished letters and from some of his lesser known works. While I have tried to resist the temptation to quote extensively from Lewis, he has often put a point so succinctly or so beautifully that it seemed better to quote than to substitute my poorer paraphrase.

My own qualifications are, first, a love of Lewis and a familiarity with almost everything written by and about him. I have read all of Lewis's published writing, some of it many times. I have read most of the books written about Lewis in English and many of the important articles. But I think that, when trying to understand a writer, one's love for that writer is fully as important as any information one might have about that writer. Understanding is a result of appreciation: hostile critics almost always more or less misread the subject of their criticism.

I am by profession a teacher and writer, a professor of philosophy at a state university and the author of ten previous books, including two fantasy novels, a number of textbooks, and a study of the fiction of Lewis and his friend J. R. R. Tolkien. I have written three books on logic and two on philosophy of religion, which gives me some qualifications for examining the strength of Lewis's arguments for Christianity. My attempts at fiction give me some grounds for appreciating Lewis's achievements in that field and the way in which he uses fiction to illuminate the ideas discussed in his nonfiction writing.

Since I agree with Lewis on most of the matters that this book deals with, some readers may find me too partial to be a good expositor of his views, preferring someone who would find more failures and faults. I must, somewhat ironically, apologize for disappointing them: I report what I find, and I find both Lewis and his case for the Christian faith worthy of respect.

The judicial metaphor of a "case" for the Christian faith is suggested by the title of one of Lewis's own books. This is the case for one side of a disputed issue: Lewis would have been, and I would be, interested in an equally detailed exposition of the other side; the case against C. S. Lewis's case for the Christian faith. But a philosopher is not an advocate; he or she must consider all of the evidence and follow the argument where it leads. If someone does not like the place where the argument has led Lewis, and myself, that person must give reasons to show that the argument should lead us elsewhere. I do not think this attempt will succeed, but I am willing to rest my case with this book and wait for the arguments on the other side.

My very special thanks to the Trustees of the Estate of C. S. Lewis, and especially to Father Walter Hooper, for permission to quote from fifteen previously unpublished letters written by Lewis. I wish to express my appreciation to Dr. Clyde Kilby and the staff of the Marion E. Wade Collection at Wheaton College, Wheaton, Illinois, for access to this fine collection of unpublished material by Lewis and for their help in making use of the material. Thanks also to the Trustees of the Lewis Estate, Collins Publishers, Macmillan Publishing Company, and Harcourt Brace Jovanovich, for permission to quote from the published works of

C. S. Lewis. I wish to thank the Bureau of Faculty Research at Western Washington University for help in the preparation of the manuscript and Robbi Burns and Mary Sutterman for typing the manuscript. Thanks also to John Shopp, Shelley Thacher, and Kathy Reigstad of Harper & Row.

1. Some Reasons for Lewis's Success

C. S. Lewis died in 1962, but his books continue to sell in the millions and to have an important influence on their readers. People as diverse as one-time Watergate coconspirator Charles Colson and former Black Panther leader Eldridge Cleaver have given Lewis's books partial credit for their return to Christianity. A few years ago, *Time* magazine's "Religion" section proclaimed that "C. S. Lewis goes marching on."[1] Recently, Lewis was cited as "this century's most-read apologist for God" in a *Time* article on renewed interest in philosophical proofs for God's existence.[2] Books by other Christian writers also sell in large numbers, but these are often books of exhortation or inspiration, addressed to those already enthusiastic about Christianity. Lewis seems to have the power to reach out to those who are skeptical or wavering, and a large number of people from very different backgrounds have given Lewis a major share of the credit for their becoming or remaining Christians.

What accounts for Lewis's extraordinary success? Those who share Lewis's beliefs might say that it was the truth of the lessons he had to teach, or the power of the Holy Spirit; but this does not explain why Lewis has been more successful than others who have taught the same lessons and invoked the same Spirit. Lewis himself was quick to say that he was only the "conductor" through which the message passed, and that "anyone or anything can be used as a conductor by the Holy Spirit."[3] But something about Lewis made him an extraordinarily effective conductor of the message he transmitted: Christianity as presented by Lewis seems to reach people in a way that Christianity as presented by other modern writers does not.

The explanation for Lewis's success is to be found in all the aspects of Lewis as a man and a writer; in his imaginative and moral qualities as well as his intellectual capacities. We will begin with his intellectual abilities. The first of these is his singular clarity, his ability to present a message so that it is comprehensible to anyone willing and able to make some intellectual effort. This was partially due to a natural talent for finding the right words for his thoughts, which more laborious writers may well envy; but it was also the result of a deliberate avoidance of jargon, an effort to speak in a way that would be understandable to the audience he was trying to reach.

When Lewis was invited to address a group of Christian teachers on how to communicate with their audience, he told them:

We must learn the language of our audience. And let me say at the outset that it is no use at all laying down *a priori* what the "plain man" does or does not understand. You have to find out by experience. . . . You must translate every bit of your Theology into the vernacular. This is very troublesome . . . but it is essential. It is also of the greatest service to your own thought. I have come to the conclusion that if you cannot translate your thoughts into uneducated language, then your thoughts are confused. Power to translate is the test of having really understood your own meaning.[4]

When he was rebuked by a scholarly theologian for using language that oversimplified the doctrines he was trying to explain, Lewis replied with gentle irony:

When I began, Christianity came before the great mass of my unbelieving countrymen either in the highly emotional form offered by revivalists or in the unintelligible language of highly cultured clergymen. Most men were reached by neither. My task was therefore simply that of a *translator*—one turning Christian doctrine . . . into the vernacular, into language that unscholarly people would attend to and could understand. . . . My manner may have been defective. Others may do better hereafter. I am ready, if I am young enough, to learn. . . . [A] more helpful critic [would] advise a cure as well as asserting many diseases. How does he himself do such work? What methods, and with what success, does he employ when he is trying to convert the great mass of storekeepers, lawyers, realtors, morticians, policemen and artisans, who surround him in his own city?

One thing at least is sure. If the real theologians had tackled this laborious work of translation about a hundred years ago, when they began to lose touch with the people (for whom Christ died) there would be no place for me.[5]

Those who hope to emulate Lewis's success may not find it easy to write with his apt choice of words, but they can certainly profit from his practice of speaking in the language appropriate to their audience. In the two passages quoted above, where Lewis is speaking to a person or persons whom he can safely assume are well educated, he uses words and turns of phrase that he would not use with a less-educated audience. It should also be emphasized that there is nothing condescending in Lewis's advice to "translate" theology into the vernacular: ordinary readers today can no more be expected to recognize the technical terms of theology than they can be expected to understand quotations given in Greek or Latin. But it is not just words that Lewis translates. Put into new words, a well-worn phrase can be fresh and illuminating (even a phrase such as "saved from our sins," which *seems* to be in everyday English, has in effect become technical terminology).

Another intellectual capacity relevant to Lewis's success was his genuine ability to listen to and understand criticisms of his own positions as well as views opposed to his own. In the above reply to a critic, Lewis says in passing: "We all know too well how difficult it is to grasp or retain the substance of a book one finds antipathetic."[6] Unfortunately, Lewis was too kind. We do not all know, or all remember, this very basic fact. A good part of many controversies consists precisely in the correction of clear misstatements by opponents of the views held by the other side. Yet, only an opponent who really understands your view can be a dangerous critic: no one is impressed by criticism that embodies plain misunderstandings of the view criticized.

Lewis had the great advantage of having himself been an opponent of Christianity and of remembering vividly not only his intellectual positions, but his feelings. As he wrote in his account of his conversion in *Surprised by Joy:*

I was at this time living, like so many Atheists or Antitheists, in a whirl of contradictions. I maintained that God did not exist. I was also very angry with God for not existing. I was equally angry with Him for creating a world.[7]

Lewis was also free of the very common vice of reading a book through the distorting lenses of his own preconceptions. He defended the idea that our *enjoyment* of a work, as well as our understanding of it, should be independent of our agreement or disagreement with the ideas expressed in that work. As he says in a work on literary criticism:

In reading imaginative works, I suggest, we should be much less concerned with altering our own opinions—though of course this is sometimes their effect—than with entering fully into the opinions, and therefore also the attitudes, feelings and total experience, of other men. Who in his ordinary senses would try to decide between the claims of materialism and theism by reading Lucretius and Dante? But who in his literary senses would not delightedly learn from them a great deal about what it is like to be a materialist or theist?

In good reading there ought to be no "problem of belief." I read Lucretius and Dante at a time when (by and large) I agreed with Lucretius. I have read them since I came (by and large) to agree with Dante. I cannot find that this has much altered my experience, or at all altered my evaluation, of either. A true lover of literature should be in one way like an honest examiner, who is prepared to give the highest works to the telling, felicitous and well-documented exposition of views he dissents from or even abominates.[8]

Even those who disagree strongly with Lewis would have to grant that he has been able, through his fiction as well as his nonfiction, to give a very good idea of "what it is like to be . . . [a] theist."

In addition to his clarity and his insight into the point of view of the opponent of Christianity, Lewis is unusual among contemporary Christian writers in that he gives *arguments* for Christianity, carrying the battle into an area that some modern Christians have seen as enemy territory. As a "Christian rationalist," Lewis held that Christianity was not merely an intellectually respectable option, not merely *as* reasonable as opposing views, but rather that Christianity was *more* reasonable than any alternative. As he says in a discussion of religious belief: "[It] is not expected that a man should assent to [Christianity] without evidence or in the teeth of the evidence. At any rate, if anyone expects that, I certainly do not. And in fact the man who accepts Christianity always thinks he has good evidence."9 Lewis himself argued in many places and in many ways that Christianity was more probable than any alternative view: more probable than the so-called "scientific world view" that is assumed to be true by most modern intellectuals, more likely to be true than any of the non-Christian religions. These arguments will be examined in detail in the following chapters.

Without prejudging whether or not Lewis was right in making these claims, we can nevertheless see that part of his popularity is due to the fact that he makes them. Many Christians, I think, have a hunger for argument and a thirst for rational justification that have not been satisfied by most contemporary Christian teachers. It may be that these longings cannot be satisfied, that Christianity is radically nonrational; but Lewis did not think so, and he convinced many of his readers that he is right.

If Lewis had only the intellectual virtues I have discussed, he would still be a formidable proponent of Christianity. But to these intellectual capacities he added an imaginative power that enabled him to illuminate and illustrate his rational insights and arguments. One way in which imagination can serve intellect is by producing metaphors to illuminate unfamiliar or difficult topics, making parallels between what needs to be understood and some familiar area of experience. Consider the following metaphor from a letter Lewis wrote in answer to his longtime friend, Arthur Greeves, who had asked whether God could understand our evil impulses, whether God in some sense "contains" or "includes" evil. Lewis begins with an analogy:

Supposing you are taking a dog on a lead* through a turnstile or past a post. You know what happens (apart from his usual ceremonies when passing a post!). He tries to go to the wrong side and gets his lead looped around the post. You see that he can't do it, and therefore pull him back. You pull him *back* because you want to enable him to go *forward.* He wants exactly the same thing—namely to go *forward:* for that very reason he resists your pull *back,* or, if he is an obedient dog, yields to it reluctantly as a matter of duty which seems to him to be quite in opposition to his own will: though *in fact* it is only by yielding to you that he will ever succeed in getting where he wants. Now if the dog were a theologian he would regard his own will as a *sin* to which he was tempted, and therefore an *evil:* and he might go on to ask whether you understood and "contained" his evil. . . . [Lewis then goes on to apply the analogy to the situation of God and human evil:] God not only understands but *shares* the desire which is at the root of all my evil: the desire for complete and ecstatic happiness. He made me for no other purpose than to enjoy it. But He knows, and I do not, how it can be really and permanently attained. He knows that most of *my* personal attempts to reach it are actually putting it further and further out of my reach. . . . Only the dog's master knows how useless it is to try to get on with the lead knotted round the lamp-post. That is why we must be prepared to find God implacably and immovably forbidding what may seem to us very small and trivial things. But He knows whether they are really small and trivial. How small some of the things that doctors forbid would seem to an ignoramus.[10]

The use of an everyday situation to illustrate a rather abstract theological question, the development of the analogy so that each detail adds to the point being made, and the touch of humor in the picture of the doggish theologian are all typical of Lewis's use of imagination in the service of argument. His writing abounds in illustrations and concrete examples, and these are often sharply observed little vignettes, like the dog winding itself around the post, or little stories in miniature. Conversely, in his fiction, we often find a real argument "transposed" into the fictional setting. For example, in Lewis's *Chronicles of Narnia,* a

---

* Americans would say "leash."

series of seven books written for children, a good many theological and philosophical points emerge very naturally in the contexts of the stories.

In one of the Narnian books, *The Silver Chair*, two children, Eustace Scrubb and Jill Pole, are traveling with a lanky and lugubrious Narnian, Puddleglum the Marshwiggle. After a series of adventures, they find themselves with a Narnian prince in an underground kingdom, confronted by a witch who tries to confuse and dismay them by pretending that their memories of the world above ground are merely dreams and fancies. A brief quotation will illustrate her method:

"What is this *sun* that you all speak of? Do you mean anything by the word? . . . Can you tell me what it's like?" asked the Witch. . . .

"Please it your Grace," said the Prince, very coldly and politely. "You see that lamp. It is round and yellow and gives light to the whole room; and hangeth moreover from the roof. Now that thing which we call the sun is like the lamp, only far greater and brighter. It giveth light to the whole Overworld and hangeth in the sky."

"Hangeth from what, my lord?" asked the Witch; and then, while they were all still thinking how to answer her, she added, with another of her soft, silver laughs, "You see? When you try to think out clearly what this *sun* must be, you cannot tell me. You can only tell me it is like the lamp. Your *sun* is a dream; and there is nothing in that dream that was not copied from the lamp. The lamp is the real thing; the *sun* is but a tale, a children's story."[11]

For children, the Witch's strategy is merely amusing or exciting (since with the help of a hypnotic drug put in the fire she almost convinces them). But the adult reading this passage can recognize the form of argument as one often used to attack religious ideas: God is merely an earthly father or ruler magnified; all the content of our idea of God is borrowed from our mundane experience. To copy the Witch's style of argument, "The father or ruler is the real thing: God is but a tale."

Since readers of *The Silver Chair* know that the sun exists and lamps are "copies" of the sun, they are in no danger of being taken in by the Witch's argument. But, as Lewis pointed out in other contexts, the general form of argument is equally suspect whether we apply it to the lamp and the sun or to the father or ruler and God. From the mere fact that A resembles B, we cannot argue that A is a copy of B *or* that B is a copy of A. The idea of God may be copied from the earthly father or ruler, but equally the earthly father or ruler may be only a faint reflection of God's fatherhood and authority. Unless we have some independent grounds for deciding, we cannot be sure which is the copy, which the original. The argument that our idea of God is only a copy of our ideas of earthly fathers or rulers assumes that this question is settled, and therefore assumes just what it ought to be proving.

I have said that Lewis "transposed" this argument to a fictional setting. The metaphor is taken from music, in which a piece of music written in one key may be transposed to another key. One of Lewis's most interesting original ideas was embodied in an essay titled "Transposition." Here Lewis starts from the fact that the bodily feelings accompanying awe or aesthetic emotion can be indistinguishable *as bodily feelings* from feelings of sickness: weakness, trembling, sensations in the pit of the stomach. If we choose to concentrate purely on physical sensations, we could make a case that awe or aesthetic emotions are "merely" a sort of sickness. Lewis argues that, in many areas of experience, we see a "higher" state "embodied in" or "transposed to" a lower one:

If the richer system is to be represented in the poorer at all, this can only be done by giving each element in the poorer system more than one meaning. . . . If you are to translate from a language which has a large vocabulary to one which has a small vocabulary, then you must be allowed to use several words in more than one sense. . . . If you are making a piano version of a piece originally scored for an orchestra, then the same piano notes which represent flutes in one passage must also represent violins in another. . . . The most familiar example of all is the art of drawing. The problem here is to represent a three-dimensional world on a flat sheet of paper. . . . The very same shape which you must draw to give the illusion of a straight road receding from the spectator is also the shape you draw for a dunce's cap.[12]

Lewis goes on to construct a parable (which reminds us of Plato's parable of the cave) of a woman thrown into a dungeon, where she bears and raises a son. Because she was an artist before her imprisonment and has managed to bring paper and drawing pencils to the dungeon, she teaches her son about the outside world by drawing pictures. But of course the son, who knows the outside world only through his mother's pictures, is bound to have misconceptions about it: he may even think that the world outside the dungeon is full of lines drawn in pencil, and when this misconception is corrected his whole notion of the outside world may become a blank. "For the lines, by which alone he was imagining it, have now been denied of it. He has no idea of that which will exclude and dispense with the lines, that of which the lines were merely a transposition—the waving tree-tops, the light dancing on the weir, the coloured three-dimensioned realities which are not enclosed in lines but define their own shapes at every moment with a delicacy and multiplicity which no drawing could ever achieve. . . ."[13]

Lewis uses the idea of transposition to cast light on such things as the relation of mind to body and the relation of the spiritual to the material world, but I wish to use it here to cast light on Lewis's own writing. In transposing such events as the death and resurrection of Christ, or the creation and end of the world to the children's stories of the Narnian chronicles, Lewis obviously loses much of the richness and complexity of the real events. At the same time, he manages to make these realities understandable to a child. Similarly, when he translates theology into everyday language, Lewis sacrifices some complexity and precision in order to make the doctrines meaningful to his audience. Every teacher, every popularizer of science or any other subject, must tread a fine line between clarification and oversimplification. Great teachers manage to make things meaningful to their audiences in terms of that audience's own experience, without losing anything essential. One of the best techniques for doing this is what Lewis called transposition, a technique of which he was a master.

When we turn from Lewis's intellectual and imaginative qualities to his moral qualities, it is his humility we notice first. Lewis
was not trying to impress his own personality on his readers or
listeners, but rather trying to get out of the way and let his
message speak. In a letter to a person who had come to him with
intellectual difficulties and who credited her eventual acceptance
of Christianity largely to him, Lewis wrote:

[As] for my part in it, remember that anybody or *anything* may be used
by the Holy Spirit as a conductor. I say this not so much for modesty as
to guard against any danger of your feeling that when the shine goes out
of my books (as it will) that the *real thing* is in any way involved. *It* won't
fade when I do.[14]

Interestingly, Lewis—who was unconcerned that his importance
might "fade," that the "shine" would go out of his books—stands
the test of time far better than authors who were concerned about
reputation: he not only continues to acquire new readers, he is
reread with profit by many of his older ones. Despite the familiarity with Lewis's work resulting from much rereading, I can still
pick up any of his books and find myself captured anew by his
style and wit.

Prominent among Lewis's other moral qualities is a deep em-
pathy, a genuine "feeling-with" those in intellectual or spiritual
difficulties. Lewis himself did not have an easy life: he lost his
mother in early childhood, was estranged from his father, and
had unhappy experiences at school. Later, he was wounded in
World War I, and had a difficult domestic life with the mother of
a comrade who died in the war. (In accordance with a promise
made to his friend Paddy Moore, Lewis "adopted" Mrs. Moore
as if she were his own mother, took her into his home, and
suffered from her domestic tyranny for many years.) When very
late in life Lewis married, his wife was already dying of cancer and
he lost her after a few years.

Both in his fiction and in his religious writing, Lewis shows the
effect of the broadened sympathies given him by his own sorrows.
Some of his most memorable fictional characters, such as Orual

in *Till We Have Faces,* are people who encounter a great deal of suffering. In *A Grief Observed,* Lewis recorded with almost clinical detachment his feelings of rebellion at the death of his wife. As he wrote to a friend, "[*A Grief Observed*] ends with faith, but raises all the blackest doubts *en route.*"[15]

A final note of Lewis's character is his enthusiastic love for so many things: books, nature, people, animals, pleasures. A typical Lewis comment is this one, in a letter to a friend: "I am lately back from Cornwall where I have been sailing for the first time. I think it is a way in which people who can't dance can get some idea of what dancing was made to give."[16] Both the enthusiasm and the apt analogy strike a characteristic Lewis note.

We might say of Lewis that he looked outward more than he looked inward. His clarity of thought he owed partly to the fact that he looked at a subject without intruding his own preconceptions. His facility of expression was due partly to a real sense of how his audience thought and felt. Most of all, his sympathy for the struggle of others arose from his having faced similar struggles.

2. Reasons for Belief in God

Christians disagree about whether reason has any place in religion at all. Some appear to believe that the weight of argument is against Christianity, but so much the worse for argument. Such Christians are fond of quoting Christ's words to the effect that God has hidden his mysteries from the "wise and prudent" and revealed them to the childlike, or St. Paul's words about "vain philosophy" and the way in which the "foolishness" of Christianity overcomes the wisdom of the world (Luke 10:21; Col. 2:8; 1 Cor. 1:17–25).

Far more common among Christians, however, is the attitude that neither Christianity nor any opposing view can be established by rational argument—that *any* view of life, any "religion" (in the broad sense in which communism and humanism are religions) requires a "leap of faith" that not only goes beyond any rational considerations, but has nothing to do with reason or argument. This view is especially popular in modern, pluralistic societies, because it seems to give a foundation to tolerance of all points of view about religion: if no religion is more reasonable than any other, then none can claim any position of privilege or find any basis for objecting to other points of view.

There remain a number of Christians, however, who take an older and bolder view: that reason is on the side of Christianity. These Christians maintain that if we begin to ask fundamental questions about the universe, and follow the argument where it leads us, then it will lead us to belief in God; that if we examine the evidence of history and of human experience, we will be compelled to acknowledge that the only satisfactory explanation of the evidence leads us to Christianity. Such Christians acknowledge that there is still a gap between intellectual assent and commitment to a Christian way of life, but they believe that reason is neither opposed to such a commitment nor irrelevant to it—rather, it is the best possible ground for it.

The middle view—which holds that all points of view about religion are equally unsupported by reason, that we can only "decide what to believe"—is so popular that many admirers of C. S. Lewis have found it possible to ignore or reject the fact that Lewis was a "rational Christian" or "Christian rationalist," who believed very strongly that we should use reason to support and explore Christianity.

To ignore that side of Lewis is to ignore something fundamental about him, something that accounts for a great deal of his influence on ordinary Christians. Where other Christian writers are valued because they can inspire or enlighten, Lewis is valued because he can convince or reinforce conviction. Many people have attributed their conversion or reconversion to Christianity in part to Lewis, and many more would credit Lewis with helping them *stay* Christians. It is precisely this argumentative side of Lewis that represents one of his main differences from the majority of contemporary Christian writers. Although it makes him unpopular in some quarters, it seems to be one of the reasons he is valued by many admirers.

It is hard to avoid the suspicion that many of the Christians who deny the value of reason and argument in religion are making a virtue of what they regard as necessity; if they thought Christianity could be victorious on the field of argument, perhaps they would be happy to embrace reason. In the past, some Protestants had strong theological reasons for distrusting reason, based on the view that the Fall or Original Sin radically corrupted all human faculties, including human reason. Today such a view is rare; in fact, it sometimes seems that many modern Christians believe that every part of human nature *except* our reasoning powers is good and can lead us to God.

In Lewis's writings, there are very few discussions of the general question of the relation of religion to reason. What comments there are on this point are generally made in passing while discussing more concrete questions. Instead, Lewis gets on with the job of arguing for Christianity. This seems to be the best way for us to proceed too. We will look at Lewis's arguments and ask if they succeed in proving what they aim to prove, rather than ask whether Lewis was right to use reason to support religion. We will begin with his arguments for belief in God, which seems to be the right place to start. Before we can ask whether Christ is the Son of God, or whether the Bible is the Word of God, surely we must have some idea that God exists and some notion of what he is like.

Many of the traditional philosophical arguments for God's existence are highly abstract and very difficult to follow. This does not mean that they are without value, but it does mean that they are a poor place to start for the ordinary person who cannot spend hours in a philosophy class examining them. One of the most abstract—yet fascinating—of the various kinds of arguments for the existence of God is the *ontological* argument. It has several varieties, all of which attempt to prove God exists by starting with the *idea* of God (unlike most other arguments, which appeal to the facts of experience, with God as an explanation of those facts).

In a letter to his brother Warren, who was then serving in the army, Lewis discusses one version of this argument:

Yes indeed: how many essays I have heard read to me on Descartes' proofs (there are more than one) of the existence of God. (It was a remark of [a friend's that] first suggested to me that God might be defined as "a Being who spends his time having his existence proved and disproved"). The particular one you quote ("I have the idea of a perfect being") seems to me to be valid or invalid according to the meaning you give the words "have an idea of." I used to work it out by the analogy of a machine. If I have the idea of a machine which I, being unmechanical, couldn't have invented on my own, does this prove that I have received the idea from some really mechanical source—i.e., a talk with the real inventor? To which I answer "Yes, if you mean a really detailed idea"; but of course there is another sense in which if a lady novelist "has an idea" of a new airship invented by her hero—in the sense that she attaches *some* vague meaning to her words, which proves nothing of the sort. So that if anyone asks one whether the idea of God in human minds proves His existence, I can only ask "*Whose* idea?" [Some people's] idea, clearly not, for it contains nothing whereof [their] own pride, fear, and malevolence could not easily provide the materials. . . . On the other hand it is arguable that the "idea of God" in *some* minds does contain, not a mere abstract definition, but real imaginative perception of goodness and beauty, beyond their own resources, and this not only in minds which already believe in God. It certainly seems to me that the "vague something" which has been suggested to one's mind as desirable, all one's life, in experiences of nature and music and poetry, even in such ostensibly irreligious forms as "the land east of the Sun and west of the Moon" in Morris, and which rouses desires that no finite object even pretends to satisfy, can be argued *not* to be any product of our own minds.[1]

Lewis was to use this general line of argument in several contexts. One of the most unusual is contained in the scene from *The Silver Chair* mentioned in the previous chapter, in which Puddlegum says to the Witch:

Suppose we *have* only dreamed, or made up, all those things—trees and grass and sun and moon and stars and Aslan himself. Suppose we have. Then all I can say is that, in that case, the made-up things seem a good deal more important than the real ones. Suppose this black pit of a kingdom of yours *is* the only world. Well, it strikes me as a pretty poor one. And that's a funny thing, when you come to think of it. We're just babies making up a game, if you're right. But four babies playing a game can make a play-world which licks your real world hollow.[2]

The line of argument suggested both in the letter and in the fictional speech is the same: if certain ideas in our minds cannot be accounted for on the basis of our experiences of the world around us—the apparently "real world"—these ideas must be accounted for in terms of something beyond the world of our experience. In the letter, Lewis suggests a divine origin for certain longings because they are desires that "no finite object even pretends to satisfy." This suggests another line of argument that we will examine later. But the letter's main argument is that the idea of God for some people contains "a real imaginative perception of goodness and beauty, beyond their own resources." Similarly, Puddlegum suggests it would be very strange if the whole idea of the real world of "trees and grass and sun and moon and stars" had no basis in reality, but was only a dream or imagination.

The argument Lewis gives is not in itself conclusive, and his opponents may be able to explain all of our ideas of God in terms of ordinary experience. But his argument is at least a challenge to anyone who denies that our ideas of God come from God himself—a challenge to show in detail, and without assuming what is supposedly being proved, where these ideas do in fact come from. This is especially a challenge to those who hold that all our ideas come from experience. By their own theories, they should be able to trace our idea of God to some experience or experiences.

We might pause here to ask if this or any of the arguments to follow shows the existence of God in the full sense. Perhaps the idea we are trying to account for was put into our minds by a being who is good but not perfectly good, powerful but not unlimited in power. To this kind of suggestion, Lewis replied:

There might be good superhuman beings of limited power (I suspect there are millions). What is this power limited by? I suppose by the general nature of things. Alright. Now is that general nature of things itself a conscious being or the work of chance? If the latter, then how did it produce the superhuman good being? Just by a lucky fluke? If the former, then a conscious being further back, the ultimate one, is what we call God and the whole problem is about *Him*. [3]

Another type of argument for God much debated by philosophers is the *cosmological* argument, which begins with certain basic features of the universe such as change, causality, or contingency, and tries to show that we can make sense of such features only in terms of God. In a letter to Bede Griffiths, a former student who became a Roman Catholic monk, Lewis said, "The Cosmological argument is, for some people at some times, ineffective. It always has been for me."[4] The scholastic philosophy that Griffiths studied as part of his preparation for the priesthood has traditionally put a good deal of weight on the cosmological argument, which is probably why it became a topic of discussion between Lewis and Griffiths. Lewis had certain misgivings about scholastic philosophy, not so much in its original development in the Middle Ages but in its modern revival, encouraged by the nineteenth-century Pope Leo XIII and some of his successors. In another letter to Griffiths, he wrote, "I hope that the great religious revival now going on will not get itself too mixed with scholasticism, for I am sure that the revival of the latter, however salutary, must be as temporary as any other movement in philosophy. Of things on the natural level now one, now another, is the ally or enemy of Faith. . . . we have no abiding city, even in philosophy: all passes except the Word."[5]

Three other arguments for God that have been debated by philosophers, and that in one form or other have convinced many people, are the *moral* argument, the argument from *religious experience,* and the argument from *design.* Lewis gave his own versions of each of these arguments, and his versions were original and important. In fact, his version of the argument from design is so original that its connection with the more traditional argument is not at all obvious.

Perhaps Lewis's version of the moral argument is most familiar to those who have read only a few of his books, for he gave it in the series of radio talks later published as *Mere Christianity*—one of his most popular nonfiction books.

He begins by pointing out that we all make moral judgments. No matter how skeptical we are about morality in theory, as soon as a moral issue enters our lives we find ourselves making judgments about rightness and wrongness. Whether it is a public issue such as the war in Vietnam, Watergate, or the American hostages in Iran, or whether it is an injustice or injury of a personal kind—a robbery, a rape, an act of cruelty done to or by someone we know—sooner or later something will cut through our theoretical moral skepticism or relativism and make us say, "That is *wrong.*" Similarly, the actions and characters of some people call forth our moral admiration, making us say, "That is *right,*" or "That person is good."

But Lewis didn't stop there. He went on to point out that all of us, when we attempt to live up to our moral ideals, find ourselves failing in the attempt. All of us recognize the claims of morality, says Lewis, and all of us must admit our failure to live up to those claims. Now all attempted explanations of these facts in nonreligious terms either fail to explain them, or explain them away. If, for example, morality is merely an instinct derived from an animal heritage, why should we obey that instinct? We try to overcome other instinctive inhibitions, such as a fear of falling, if such inhibitions get in the way of what we want to do. On the other hand, our attitude towards the rapist or the hostage-taker is not that they have overcome inhibitions that still hold us captive, but that they are doing something they ought not to be doing.

Lewis argues that only the traditional idea of a God who is the source of the moral order, and a human race estranged from that God, can explain both elements of the facts: our recognition of morality and of our own failure to live up to it. Here we are reminded of his argument about the idea of God, for here again is something in our experience that resists efforts at explanation in naturalistic terms, but makes perfectly good sense in terms of traditional Christian belief in God. Our idea of God contains elements of goodness and beauty beyond our natural capacities because it comes from God; our moral experience contains demands that we feel to be just, because those demands come from the creator of our nature; we fail to live up to those demands because we are estranged from our creator.

The situation is not quite the same for the opponents of the moral argument as for the opponents of the argument about the idea of God, who may simply argue that we can explain away our idea of God naturalistically. For if Lewis is right in saying that naturalistic explanations of morality rob morality of its force, then the opponent of the moral argument has a dilemma. To get rid of God the opponent must get rid of morality—a price not all of us are willing to pay.

The argument for God from religious experience may appeal to very special experiences, of a kind which very few people have, or experiences that are common to many people. The second appeal seems to be the stronger one, but very often the discussion of religious experience gets bogged down in the complications of those rare and special religious experiences that are often called mystical experiences, in which certain unusual individuals seem to have had some kind of direct contact with a reality beyond everyday experience. Lewis tended to be skeptical about appeals to such experiences in religious argument and did not himself make use of them. He wrote in *Letters to Malcolm:*

One thing common to all mysticisms is the temporary shattering of our ordinary spatial and temporal consciousness and of our discursive intellect. The value of this negative experience must depend on the nature of that positive, whatever it is, for which it makes room. But should we not expect that the negative would always *feel* the same? . . . All who leave the land and put to sea will "find the same things"—the land sinking below the horizon, the gulls dropping behind, the salty breeze. Tourists, merchants, sailors, pirates, missionaries—it's all one. But this identical experience vouches for nothing about the utility or unlawfulness or final event of their voyages.

It may be that the gulfs will wash them down,
It may be that they will touch the Happy Isles.

I do not at all regard mystical experience as an illusion. I think it shows that there is a way to go, before death, out of what may be called "this world"—out of the stage set. Out of this; but into what? That's like asking an Englishman, "Where does the sea lead to?" He will reply, "To everywhere on earth, including Davy Jones's locker, except England." The lawfulness, safety, and utility of the mystical voyage depends not at all on its being mystical—that is, on its being a departure—but on the motives, skill, and constancy of the voyager, and on the grace of God. The true religion gives value to its own mysticism; mys-

ticism does not validate the religion in which it happens to occur.
I shouldn't be at all disturbed if it could be shown that a diabolical
mysticism, or drugs, produced experiences indistinguishable (by intro-
spection) from those of the great Christian mystics. Departures are all
alike; it is the landfall that crowns the voyage. The saint, by being a saint,
proves that his mysticism (if he was a mystic; not all saints are) led him
aright; the fact that he has practised mysticism could never prove his
sanctity.[6]

Descriptions of mystical experience are rare in contemporary
literature, and many people may have little idea of what such
experiences are like. Lewis provides an interesting "transposition" of mystical experience into imaginatively appealing terms
in his novel *That Hideous Strength,* when he is attempting to give
an imaginative insight into the mental processes of Mr. Bultitude,
a bear who plays a part in the story:

Mr. Bultitude's mind was as furry and inhuman in shape as his body.
. . . There was no prose in his life. The appetites which a human mind
might disdain as cupboard loves were for him quivering and ecstatic
aspirations which absorbed his whole being, infinite yearnings stabbed
with the threat of tragedy and shot through with the colors of Paradise.
One of our race, if plunged back for a moment in the warm, trembling
iridescent pool of that pre-Adamite consciousness would have emerged
believing that he had grasped the Absolute: for the states below reason
and the states above it have, by their common contrast to the life we
know, a certain superficial resemblance. . . . He felt, in his own fashion,
the supremacy of the Director. Meetings with him were to the bear what
mystical experiences are to men. . . . In his presence Mr. Bultitude
trembled on the very borders of personality, thought the unthinkable,
did the impossible, was troubled by gleams from beyond his own woolly
world, and came away tired. . . .[7]

(The Director is a character in the story who, for reasons that
do not concern us here, has special rapport with animals and
"some shadow of man's lost prerogative to ennoble beasts.")
The description of mystical experience that emerges indirectly
from this passage is an interesting one: "quivering and ecstatic
aspirations which [absorb the] whole being, infinite yearn-

ings. . . ." The bear's meetings with the Director are analogous to a human's mystical union with God, and the effect is to raise the creature to a level higher than that on which it normally functions—almost to a human level. The analogous experience for a human would be to function, however partially and tenuously on a superhuman, even a divine level. Some mystics have described the experience in terms very much like this and Lewis, of course, was drawing on his wide reading of the classics of Christian mysticism.

But he was also drawing on experiences of his own, which he felt almost everyone shared to some extent, and he used them as the basis of an argument for religious belief. He gave these experiences the somewhat misleading name of "joy" in his spiritual autobiography *Surprised by Joy;* but, as his description of the experiences shows, they were mainly experiences of intense *longing,* which could not be satisfied by any finite object. In fact, "joy" is a more ordinary and less intense version of the mystic's "ecstatic aspirations . . . infinite yearnings."

Lewis argues in a number of places, including Book III, Chapter II of *Mere Christianity,* that such longings are indicative of a real need that must surely have a real object. Hunger is natural: food, which is its object, exists. Sexual desire is normal: sexual satisfaction is possible. And if there is in our nature a desire for something that no finite object will satisfy, then we can argue that something exists that will satisfy that longing. The inference is not certain, but it is overwhelmingly probable: longings do not arise unless they can be satisfied.

Someone who wanted to object to this argument might reply with the modern view that "divine dissatisfaction," a constant search for something beyond what we have, is a characteristic valuable for survival. Thus its existence and persistence can be explained on grounds of evolution by natural selection. The price one pays for taking this line is that it makes the desires in question unsatisfiable in principle. If our "infinite longings" do not mean that an infinite object exists to satisfy them, then they mean that we shall never be satisfied.

Some might argue that this is not a bad thing, that "to travel hopefully is better than to arrive." But to travel *hopefully* surely means to travel with the hope of arriving at a satisfactory destination. Once you give up the hope of a destination you may still travel for the sake of travel, still "enjoy the trip," but you can hardly be said to travel *hopefully*. And without hope of reaching a satisfactory end, is the journey all that desirable? "To travel hopefully is better than to arrive" is, in fact, a cynic's maxim; a way of saying that all destinations fall short of our hopes. But if we believe that, we cease to travel hopefully. In plainer language, an intense aspiration that we *know* cannot be satisfied is painful, not enjoyable.

Again, we can see a familiar pattern lurking in this argument; it is possible to resist the pull toward God in our religious experience (as in our moral experience); but if we do so we invalidate those experiences themselves. One of Lewis's ruling principles is that to reject God is to reject every good thing, and to accept any good thing is to put our feet on the path that leads to God. This is as true in the realm of argument towards God as it is true in the realm of living up to a commitment to God once we have made it.

The last and most complex of Lewis's arguments for God is one that *Time* magazine dubbed "The Mental Proof." An article published in April 1980, entitled "Modernizing the Case for God" and subtitled "Philosophers refurbish the tools of reason to sharpen arguments for theism," discussed the current philosophical revival of arguments for God by the present generation of philosophers. The article summarizes a number of the arguments we have discussed. The section headed "The Mental Proof" reads as follows:

In this formulation an all-intelligent Being is offered as the only explanation for the power of reason and for humanity's other nonmaterial qualities of mind and imagination. A contemporary restatement is the 1947 classic *Miracles* by the late English literary critic C. S. Lewis, the century's most read apologist for God. Lewis dismissed the philosophy that mind results from nature: "If any thought is valid an eternal, self-existent Reason must exist and must be the source of my own imperfect and intermittent rationality."[8]

In typical journalistic fashion, *Time* has given the *conclusion* of Lewis's argument without giving any clue as to the argument itself. One way of getting a preliminary insight into Lewis's argument is to ask whether nature is a product of mind, or mind is a product of nature. If God created nature, as Christians believe, then nature is understandable by reason because it is a product of reason. It sounds superficially plausible to say that if mind is the product of nature, nature would be understandable by mind as well. But in fact, there is no acceptable general rule that a product can understand what produces it.

Furthermore, if nature is seen as nonrational, as without intelligence or purpose of its own, a special difficulty arises. One thing may produce another by design, by chance, or by some process that unfolds or develops what is already inherent in the producing agent. I produced the words on this page of my manuscript by design. In doing so, I produced a random pattern of letters in the left-hand margin. If you had the manuscript page before you and found any words spelled out by reading down the first letter in each line, those words would be there purely by chance. (Since this page will be set in type after I have written it, another random factor is introduced; I have no idea if the first letters of the lines on the resulting book page will form any words.) As I was writing, my body was producing blood, digestive juices, and other secretions by a process determined by my biological makeup.

If nature is without intelligence or purpose, it cannot produce mind by design. If there is no intelligence or purpose in nature, then it cannot produce mind as the unfolding or development of something already there. So a mindless nature could produce mind only by chance. But if mind is only a chance product of nature, how can we trust our reasoning powers, how can we expect our minds to give us the truth about anything? To use a more contemporary analogy, would you trust the results of a computer that had been constructed or programmed by some random process?

In his original statement of this argument in *Miracles,* Lewis overstated his case slightly, saying that as soon as we find that a thought or belief results from chance we immediately discount or disregard that thought or belief. Lewis used the example of a belief, produced by a childhood trauma, that dogs are dangerous. As a matter of practical reasoning, it is certainly true that we discount a belief if we discover it originates in chance, but as a matter of logic it does not follow that the belief is false. It might happen that the belief is true, as a matter of chance, just as it might happen as a matter of chance that the letters on the left-hand margin of this page spell out the correct answer to some question. One cannot rule out the possibility though one ignores it for practical purposes.

It is sometimes alleged that Lewis's argument on this point was refuted in a famous debate with the Cambridge philosopher Elizabeth Anscombe. In fact, what happened was that Anscombe pointed out the overstatement we have discussed, and in typical philosopher's fashion challenged him to define some of his key terms. Lewis may indeed have been nonplussed at the vigor of her attack and its source, since as a Catholic she might have been expected to be an ally. The result of her challenge was that Lewis rewrote the chapter of *Miracles* in which the argument occurs, clarifying and strengthening the argument.[9]

Nevertheless, the emendation of the argument makes no practical difference. Suppose that you accepted a demonstration ride on a new computer-controlled airplane, only to be told that the plane's computer had been programmed with computer cards that had been randomly punched by a football player who walked over them in spiked shoes. You would not be greatly reassured by being told that the random process *might* have programmed the computer to fly the plane safely, that this was a logical possibility.

Critics of this argument would reply that, however unlikely in principle it is that a chance process should create reason, it seems to have happened, for we do know that we can trust our reason. Indeed, Lewis did not question that we must take the reliability of reason as a fixed datum. But to say that, because reason exists, chance must have brought it into existence, is to beg the question. When we have to choose between two explanations of an event, one that makes it probable and another that makes it extremely improbable, the reasonable person will always choose the explanation that makes the event probable.

For instance, suppose you encounter a plausible stranger who persuades you to bet with him on the tosses of a coin, and you choose to bet on heads; tails come up time after time, and you lose quite a lot of money. It is possible that the coin is a fair one and the stranger has won your money honestly; but it is far more likely that the coin or the toss is rigged in some way. As tails come up time after time, and the chances that this would happen with a fair coin grow tinier and tinier, the alternate explanation is more and more likely. Similarly, the chance that intelligence was produced by a random process is so small that the alternate hypothesis—that "an eternal, self-existent Reason must exist and must be the source of my own imperfect and intermittent reason" —is the reasonable choice.

The suggestion that reason was produced by natural selection is often introduced at this point. Natural selection is the process by which small random variations in the characteristics of animals tend to be passed on to those animals' descendants if they are favorable to survival. For example, the currently accepted theory about the origin of the eye is that the accumulation of small changes over a period of millennia transformed what was originally a skin area sensitive to light into the intricate optical mechanism now found in humans and animals.

Since such facts as the intricacy of the human eye were a favorite starting point for some versions of the design argument for the existence of God, the success of the natural selection theory seemed to strike a fatal blow at this sort of argument. But when we attempt to use as an explanation of the existence of intelligence itself natural selection, Lewis points out some difficulties:

This argument works only if there are such things as heredity, the struggle for existence, and elimination. But we know about these things —certainly about their existence in the past—only by inference. Unless, therefore, you start by assuming inference to be valid you cannot know about them. You have to assume that inference is valid before you can even begin your argument for its validity. And a proof which sets out by assuming the thing you have to prove is rubbish. But waive that point. Let heredity and the rest be granted. Even then you cannot show that our processes of thought yield truth unless you are allowed to argue "Because a thought is useful, therefore it must be at least partly true." But this is itself an inference. If you trust it you are once more assuming that very validity which you set out to prove.[10]

Here, I think Lewis makes one of his rare missteps in argument. Both Lewis and the "naturalist" can be seen as taking the trustworthiness of reason as a given, and seeking an explanation for that agreed-upon fact. The naturalist's explanation is evolution; Lewis's explanation is that our reason is derived from the divine reason. What Lewis needs to argue, and indeed does argue indirectly, is that it is overwhelmingly more probable that mind will be produced by a previously existing mind than by a process such as evolution, which only selects characteristics favorable to survival under the conditions prevailing at a given time. As Lewis says, on the evolutionist's account:

[Reason] is a behavior evolved simply as an aid to practice. That is why when we use it as an aid to practice we get along fairly well but when we fly off into speculation and try to get general views of "reality" we end in the endless, useless and probably merely verbal disputes of the philosopher. We will be humbler in future. Goodbye to all that. No more theology, no more ontology, no more metaphysics. . . . But then equally, no more Naturalism. For of course Naturalism is a prime specimen of that towering speculation, divorced from practice and going far beyond experience which is now being condemned.[11]

I said earlier that Lewis's "mental proof" was a form of the design argument. Some versions of the argument, such as the one that so intricate a mechanism as the eye must have had a designer, have been at least weakened by the alternate explanation offered by natural selection. Other versions ask why, if nature is nonrational, it is apparently orderly and understandable to the human mind—why there are "laws of nature" at all. These are untouched by natural selection theories, for natural selection operates only in the biological realm—and then only when certain preconditions (inheritance, population pressure, and random mutation) are present. But Lewis's argument goes even deeper, focusing on the human faculty that discovers the laws of nature and shows that God can account for that, whereas "naturalism" cannot.

Or rather, if naturalism does explain reason, it explains it away, robbing us of our confidence in reason. This repeats the pattern we have seen in Lewis's previous arguments: we can reject belief in God only at the cost of rejecting all the fundamentals of human life—our hopes of satisfaction for our "infinite longings," our moral certainties, and finally reason itself.

3. What Must God Be Like?

For many people today, the problem to be faced is not that of God's existence. It hardly occurs to them that this is desirable, much less possible. For them, the difficulty is one of having any adequate idea of God. Thus they have very little interest in the question of whether or not God exists. A great many people, even otherwise quite intelligent and well-educated people, have an idea of God that is either so primitive or so abstract—or is such a curious mixture of both—that it gives them no help at all in thinking about God.

By a primitive idea of God, I mean first of all an anthropomorphic one: the picture of an old man with a white beard enthroned on a cloud somewhere in the sky. When one of the Russian cosmonauts said with apparent seriousness that he had not encountered God in his space trips, this seems to have been his picture of God. But aside from anthropomorphism in that physical sense, many people seem to think of God as having human characteristics and human limitations. No doubt this is sometimes due to misunderstood or half-remembered biblical imagery, and many who believe this probably realize this primitive idea of God is not held by the Christians they know. But even so, the image has its effect. As the senior devil, Screwtape, says to the junior devil, Wormwood, in *The Screwtape Letters:* "Suggest to [the person you are tempting] a picture of something in red tights and persuade him that since he cannot believe in that . . . he therefore can't believe in you."[1] This is a ploy for persuading moderns not to believe in devils, and a similar ploy seems to have its effect on belief in God: "Suggest to them a picture of an old man enthroned on a cloud and persuade them that since they can't believe in that they can't believe in God."

At the opposite extreme is a picture so abstract and remote as to kill interest: God as a "force" or "power" somehow "behind" or "before" the universe. About this Lewis said, "Never . . . let us think that while anthropomorphic images are a concession to our weakness the abstractions are the literal truth. Both are equally concessions; each singly misleading and the two together mutually corrective. Unless you sit to it very lightly . . . the abstraction is fatal. It will make the life of lives inanimate and the love of loves impersonal . . . ."[2]

Lewis himself always emphasized the intense *personality* of God: not only is God a person, he is the only *real* person; our personhood is a pale and remote shadow of God's. Since for some people "being a person" seems to mean "having a body," it may be worthwhile to explain what Lewis meant (and what traditional theologians and philosophers meant) by being a person. A person is a being capable of *knowing* and *choosing*. (A baby may not *yet* be making choices, a person in a coma may not *now* be making choices, but both are *capable* of knowing and choosing.) God has both knowledge and choice in the highest degree, always aware of everything capable of being known, and able to choose perfectly. God's choices are always morally perfect but otherwise completely unimpeded: God can choose anything but evil, and his choices determine what occurs in reality.

Perfect knowledge, or *omniscience;* unimpeded choice, or *omnipotence;* and morally perfect choice, or *perfection*—these are the defining characteristics of God in traditional theology and philosophy. If God were not aware, if he were unable to choose, then God would be *sub*personal: less than we are. But, in fact, God is *super*personal: all that we are, and far more. The primitive idea of God takes away God's superpersonality to substitute a human personality; the abstract idea of God takes away personality altogether.

The modern person sometimes asks, "Why should I care about God?" The first step in answering is to point out that if the traditional idea of God is true, we would cease to exist if God did not think of us and will to keep us in existence. God is interested in us; that in itself is a reason. Think of some person you admire intensely; imagine that person wanted you to get to know him or her better: would you not respond? (If you admire no one you are in a bad way; but if you think, "I'd rather get to know N than God," recall that God *invented* N.)

Lewis's vivid sense of the "personalness" of God is due partly to his poetic, insightful side, but it is founded on his logical, analytic side. A difficult and seemingly remote theological and philosophical idea takes on new splendor and relevance in the light of his insight. Consider a problem that has bothered many believers: if God knows everything, then God knows the future. But if God knew yesterday what I will do tomorrow, how can I be free, as I believe I am, to do or not to do certain things tomorrow?

This is a genuine problem that will not yield to simple solutions. If what is in the past cannot be changed, and if God's knowledge of my future actions is in the past, then God's knowledge of those actions cannot change. But if God's knowledge of those actions cannot be changed, then those actions cannot be changed. Thus, what I will do in the future is unchangeably settled and I have no power to alter it. I am not free with regard to anything I cannot alter, and thus I have no freedom with regard to any of my actions (all of my actions were once in the future).

Some Christians have accepted this consequence, but at a terrible cost. For if I am not free, I am not responsible; and if I am not free with regard to any of my actions, I am not responsible for any of them—including any of my sins. It is unjust to punish a person for something he or she is not responsible for, so if God punishes me for my sins then God is unjust. In fact, if we accept God's omniscience, the existence of suffering seems to become a problem, for Christians usually explain suffering in terms of free choice. Thus, two ideas basic to Christianity, God's omniscience on the one hand and human freedom and responsibility on the other, seem incompatible.

In his writings, Lewis discussed this problem several times. There is a long and careful discussion in a chapter titled "Time and Beyond Time" in *Mere Christianity,* and a characteristically witty discussion in *Screwtape* Letter 27.[3] In both the solution is the one given by the Christian philosopher Boethius in the fifth century A.D.: God is not "in time" the way we are. God is *outside* of time and does not *fore*see the future; rather, he *sees* it in an "eternal now" that is equally present to all parts of time. God did not know *yesterday* what I *will* do tomorrow; he sees timelessly in eternity "what I am doing" in the future just as he sees what I am doing now. (Of course the present tense for the future sounds inappropriate, but it is the least misleading way of speaking.)

This idea has been challenged by philosophers who argued that we cannot make sense of the idea of God's timelessness or of an "eternal now." Lewis himself was careful to call the idea a philosophical theory, not a part of essential Christian belief. Certainly, we are stretching the very limits of thought and language by trying to imagine a timeless mode of existence. We must be careful not to conclude that since past, present, and future are equally present to God, they are equally present to each other. Both space and time are real, not just illusions, but God created them both and is not bound by either.

Lewis tries to convey the idea imaginatively by asking us to think of a novelist and his or her characters. The novelist is not bound by the time sequence in the novel; between two events that occur within seconds of each other in the novel, the novelist can pause for hours or days.

Even if the idea of God's timelessness is not meaningful, we still have a way out of the difficulty. While God must know everything knowable, perhaps it is not possible to know in advance the actions of a truly free being. By giving us freedom, God would have given up some possibilities of knowledge, just as leaving us free puts certain restrictions on God's power. I cannot *both* leave you free and control your actions; one choice logically excludes the other. Making us free and responsible was a partial abdication of power by God; perhaps it was also a partial abdication of knowledge.

This need not mean that God has no more idea of the future than we do. If the future is in a constant state of change as free beings make new choices, it may be this constantly changing future that God knows. God can intervene when necessary, to secure some particular result. Although a novice chessplayer playing with a master is perfectly free to move as he or she wills, the master player can easily control the course of the game. Lewis, who was satisfied with Boethius's solution, does not explore this one; but it is clear that, given a choice between abandoning freedom and modifying a certain idea of God's knowledge, he would modify the theory about God's knowledge.

It is true that certain biblical passages seem to suggest a timeless God in whom there is no change, but Lewis was skeptical about basing theological doctrines on scriptural metaphors:

All we can really substitute for the analogical expressions is some theological abstraction . . . our abstract thinking is itself an issue of analogies . . . what they now call "de-mythologising" Christianity can easily be "re-mythologising" it—substituting a poorer mythology for a richer.[4]

Part of this remythologizing may lead us to the absurdly anthropomorphic idea of God as a harried executive, the "manager" of the universe who cannot possibly remember details such as our insignificant selves: the sort of God, as Lewis said once, who if he wished to consider some "case" would have to say, "Gabriel, get me Mr. Lewis's file!"

The idea of the "managerial" God gets in our way, and makes us think that God couldn't possibly be personally interested in such insignificant persons as ourselves. But actually, God, having created each one of us and having to keep us in existence knows each of us intimately and cares about each of us intimately, just as a good novelist knows and cares about each of his or her characters. When, following Lewis, I said something to this effect to a novelist with whom I was corresponding, she replied, "People have often asked me how I keep in mind and control the many people in my 'secondary world,' and when this was first put to me I thought it rather a silly question. I wanted to answer, 'I made the thing; I *know* it and it requires no effort to keep it in mind and control it.' You will probably think me naive for never previously thinking of the Creator of the universe in this faint but illuminating light of my own experience."

Lewis's general principle, as you will notice in the quotation, is that when there is an apparent conflict between abstract ideas derived from theorizing about God and the images given to us in Scripture, it is the theoretical abstractions that must go; the scriptural images have far more depth, far more nourishment for our minds. Does this appeal to Scripture conflict with Lewis's appeal to reason in his arguments for God's existence? Lewis would have said "no: once we are convinced that God exists, it is natural to ask whether he has done anything to tell us 'what God is like.' " In the Old and New Testaments, Lewis argued, we have the best examples of such self-revelation by God. If we can give good arguments for the authenticity of this revelation, it is entirely rational to appeal to it, just as when we become convinced that a teacher or a reference book is reliable it is rational to trust what we learn from that source.

A good many objections to Christian belief seem to come from people who have totally ignored the scriptural basis of Christian belief and made up their own versions of what Christians believe. The immense amount of suffering and moral evil in the world has prevented many people from believing in a good and loving God, and indeed it does present difficulties for the believer, though perhaps not quite the difficulties the unbeliever imagines. Very often, objections to God based on suffering and evil seem to assume that a loving God wouldn't permit suffering and sin, so Christians ought to expect a world without sin and suffering and ought to be dismayed by their existence.

But if we look away from what their opponents think Christians ought to believe to what Christians do believe, we see that we are constantly being told by Scripture and by the great Christian teachers to expect suffering and to be glad of the opportunity it offers: to expect sin in ourselves and others and to work to overcome it.

Christians believe that this world is not our home but our

testing ground; that we can be eternally happy if we accept God, and eternally unhappy if we reject God. Some suffering is certainly directed to keeping us from making ourselves too much at home in the world, in order to turn us back to God, the only permanent source of happiness. In *The Problem of Pain*, Lewis wrote:

Everyone has noticed how hard it is to turn our thoughts to God when everything is going well with us. We "have all we want" is a terrible saying when "all" does not include God. We find God an interruption. . . . Now God, who has made us, knows what we are and that our happiness lies in Him. Yet we will not seek it in Him as long as He leaves us any other resort where it can even plausibly be looked for. While what we call "our own life" remains agreeable we will not surrender it to Him. What then can God do in our interests but make "our own life" less agreeable to us, and take away the plausible source of false happiness? It is just here, where God's providence seems at first to be most cruel, that the Divine humility, the stooping down of the Highest, most deserves praise. We are perplexed to see misfortune falling upon decent, inoffensive, worthy people—on capable, hard-working mothers of families or diligent, thrifty, little trades-people, on those who have worked so hard, and so honestly, for their modest stock of happiness and now seem to be entering on the enjoyment of it with the fullest right. How can I say with sufficient tenderness what here needs to be said? . . . Let me implore the reader to try to believe, if only for the moment, that God, who made these deserving people, may really be right when He thinks that their modest prosperity and the happiness of their children are not enough to make them blessed: that all this must fall from them in the end, and that if they have not learned to know Him they will be wretched. And therefore He troubles them, warning them in advance of an insufficiency that one day they will have to discover. The life of themselves and their families stands between them and the recognition of their need; He makes that life less sweet to them.[5]

Or, as Lewis put it in a letter to a friend who was an Anglican nun, "What God wants of us is a cheerful insecurity."[6]

Some suffering is certainly the direct result of our own sins: we have brought it on ourselves, we deserve it. It will be well for us if we can learn from it, but if we refuse to learn from the suffering our sins bring to us, perhaps others will. Some suffering brought on us by the sins of others is certainly the price we pay for being part of the human community. From membership in society we derive immense benefits, things we could never have brought about ourselves: books, music, art and architecture, all the scientific discoveries and the technological marvels that make our lives so easy. But just as we benefit from the good that others do, we suffer from the evil that they do; and some of this seems a reasonable price for the advantages of living in the human community.

When all this has been said, however, there seems to be a stubborn remainder of suffering that on the face of it is unfair or excessive: seemingly useless suffering. It cannot be emphasized too strongly that a clear-headed Christian like Lewis would quite agree with opponents of Christianity that if God allows any *really* useless suffering, any suffering that does no good at all, then God would not be perfectly good. What the Christian does is try to show that we have stronger reasons for believing that God is good, and therefore no suffering is really useless, than we have for believing that some suffering is useless. The most difficult problem is extreme suffering in infants and young children, who certainly have no guilt deserving of such terrible punishment, and who seem to have no need for such suffering to bring them away from the world and back to God.

But one of the most basic tenets of the Christian religion is the idea that the sufferings of a completely good and innocent person, Christ, have "saved" or "redeemed" sinful humanity. If we can see the sufferings of other good and innocent persons as somehow part of this redemptive process, then we have an answer in principle to the problem of the suffering of the good and innocent. Once we look at Christianity in this light, we can see that it is full of pointers toward this solution. The idea of the church as the Body of Christ, the canonization of the martyrs, the exhortations in the Gospel and Epistles to rejoice when we are found *worthy* to suffer, all point in this direction. In the days after Christmas, the church to which Lewis belonged celebrates a day dedicated to St. Stephen, the first Christian martyr, who imitated

Christ by praying for forgiveness for those who killed him, and a day dedicated to the "Holy Innocents," the babies who were killed when Herod tried to kill the infant Jesus.

In *The Problem of Pain,* written soon after his reconversion to Christianity, Lewis had little to say about this distinctively Christian answer to the problem of suffering. Later in life, in a letter written in 1951, Lewis said:

> I have not a word to say against the doctrine that Our Lord suffers in all the suffering of his people (see Acts IX.6) or that when we willingly accept what we suffer for others and offer it to God on their behalf, then it may be united with His sufferings and, in Him, may help in their redemption or even that of others whom we do not dream of. So that it is not in vain: though of course we must not count on seeing it work out exactly as we, in our present ignorance, might think best. The key test for this view is Colossians 1:24. Is it not, after all, one more application of the truth that we are all "members one of another"? I wish I had known more when I wrote *Problem of Pain. . . .*[7]

The two New Testament texts that Lewis cites are especially important for understanding the Christian view in question. In Acts 9:3–5, an account is given of St. Paul's conversion on the road to Damascus: "A light from heaven shone brightly about him. He fell to the ground and heard a voice saying to him, 'Saul, Saul, why are you persecuting me?' 'Who are you, Lord?' he asked. 'Jesus, who Saul persecutes,' was the reply." Jesus, of course, had been crucified some time before; it was not Christ in his own body that Saul persecuted, but Christ in his mystical body, the Christian community. The important point here is that the sufferings of members of Christ's mystical body are identified as part of the sufferings of Christ.

That this extends to many persons who are not aware of suffering *for* Christ is made clear in the traditional attitude towards the Holy Innocents, the Jewish children who were killed when Herod, in an attempt to wipe out what he saw as a challenge to his throne, "issued orders, and killed all male children of two years old and under in Bethlehem and the surrounding district"

(Matt. 2:16). Christian tradition has always regarded these children as martyrs, and their feast is celebrated soon after Christmas. Plainly, these children were not conscious martyrs for Christ; they can be regarded as representatives of all those innocents who have suffered as the result of sin, whose suffering is incorporated into Christ's redemptive suffering.

The other text that Lewis cites is in a letter of St. Paul. The Apostle says, "Even as I write I am glad of my sufferings on your behalf, as in this mortal frame of mine I help to pay off the debt which the afflictions of Christ still leave to be paid, for the sake of his body the Church" (Col. 1:24, Knox). Although the text has been translated in various ways, the Apostle's claim that his own sufferings go together with Christ's sufferings to "pay off the debt" of sin cannot be translated away. Some Christians may find troubling the suggestion that Christ's sufferings "still leave to be paid" anything necessary for redemption, and this may be Pauline hyperbole. But that our sufferings *contribute* to redemption for others is the plain sense of this and other scriptural passages.

Of course, some non-Christians find unintelligible or repellent the whole idea of one person's suffering helping to redeem another person. But the argument from evil against the existence of God is supposed to show an inconsistency in the Christian position: "You Christians believe in a loving God. How can you reconcile this with the suffering in the world?" If within their world view Christians have an explanation for suffering, they can refute the charge of inconsistency. Whether or not their explanation is true depends on the reliability of the sources from which they draw it—a question we will consider in a later chapter.

So far, we have not said anything directly about why God permits sin. The answer given by mainstream Christianity, and also by Lewis, is that God wants our freely given love and obedience. For us to be able to give God our love and obedience freely we must *be* free, and if we are free we are able to sin. The relation of free will to sin can be puzzling: why did God give us freedom if he knew we would misuse it? As Lewis wrote to an inquirer:

I do feel very strongly the difficulty you raise, "If man fell, then man must be made of poor stuff, and why did God make him so?" But then I am always pulled up by realizing that when I am arguing this way I am actually denying freedom. We are saying, "If he fell he was made of poor stuff." Does that imply "If he had been made of good stuff he could not have fallen"? If not the whole argument collapses: for if a creature made of good stuff *could* fall the fact of man's falling does not prove he was made of bad stuff. If so (i.e. if it does imply this) then we are saying that a really good creature would be incapable of moral choice—which is almost saying, "A good creature means a creature incapable of real goodness." For surely power to be good and to be bad go together, and when you remove one you remove the other? E.g. take away a creature's sexuality and you have made not only chastity but unchastity impossible for it. Every new faculty opens up new possibilities both of good and of evil. I don't think that we show any particular *personal* stupidity in forgetting this: the truth is that freedom and choice, though we all believe in them are strictly incomprehensible to the human mind. You start by admitting them: but when one tries to think of them one always lets them slip through one's fingers.[8]

Once the human race set off on the path of sin, it became harder for each individual to resist sin. That is an essential part of the doctrine of Original Sin: we inherit from our sinful ancestors a human nature more inclined to sin than human nature was when God made it. Lewis did not share the idea held by some Protestants that human nature is so "totally depraved" by Original Sin that our natural powers are no use at all for leading us to God. But he did hold, along with the majority of traditional Christians, that we need special help from God to be worthy of the wonderful destiny of sharing God's life. The technical term for this help is "grace" or "sanctifying grace." As Lewis said in a letter, "I have avoided the *term* 'Grace' but the thing itself I have dealt with in at least a rough and ready way."[9]

Christians have argued whether our salvation and reformation is due entirely to God's help or grace, or whether our own efforts play some essential part. Lewis pointed out that Scripture often seems to give both answers: "Work out your own salvation in fear and trembling" seems to put it all on our own efforts; but the next verse, "for it is God who works in you," emphasizes God's part (Phil. 2:12). Lewis pictured the situation as one in which God is continually battering on our defenses, asking us to open our hearts. But God will not enter without our consent; we have the power to say "no." Once we do say "yes," we can say that what happens after that is due to God; but until we say yes he respects our freedom and will not—we might even say cannot—save us.

This raises the issue of what will happen if we *never* give our consent, keep God out of our hearts throughout our whole existence. The traditional answer, which Lewis accepted sorrowfully, is hell: a state of final and total separation from God. Lewis says in *The Problem of Pain:*

> Some will not be redeemed. There is no doctrine which I would more willingly remove from Christianity than this, if it lay in my power. But it has the full support of Scripture and, specially, of Our Lord's own words; it has always been held by Christendom; and it has the support of reason. . . . If the happiness of a Christian lies in self surrender, no one can make that sacrifice but himself (though many can help him to make it) and he may refuse. I would pay any price to be able to say truthfully, "All will be saved." But my reason retorts "With their will or without it?" If I say "Without their will" I at once perceive a contradiction: how can the supreme voluntary act of self-surrender be involuntary? If I say "With their will" my reason replies "How if they *will not* give in?"[10]

Some great Christian teachers have held the universalist doctrine that all human beings will eventually be saved. One of these was George MacDonald, of whom Lewis said, "I have always regarded him as my master." Other Christians have speculated that those who finally refuse obedience to God will eventually be destroyed, rather than remain in some state of endless pain. The chief image used in Scripture for hell, that of fire, may suggest this, for the normal action of fire is to eventually consume what it burns. Those who have held this destructionist position have even pointed out that Christ's most definite words about the duration of hell, "where the worm dies not and the fire is not quenched" (Mark 9:48), seem to refer to the eternal quality of the means of punishment rather than of the duration of time souls are punished.

However, neither destructionism nor universalism has been widely accepted by Christians, and Lewis thought it only honest to give the best defense he could of the majority doctrine.

Once it is seen that the suffering of those who go to hell would be due not to some arbitrary command of God, but rather to their own stubborn refusal to accept life and love, a good many objections are answered. Perhaps one still remains: how can those in heaven enjoy their bliss if they know that others are suffering hell? In *The Great Divorce,* Lewis puts an answer to this question into the mouth of George MacDonald, whose spirit appears as a character in the story. Lewis has MacDonald say:

> That sounds very merciful, but see what lurks behind it. . . . The demand of the loveless and self-imprisoned that they should be allowed to blackmail the universe: that until they consent to be happy (on their own terms) no one else shall taste joy; that theirs should be the final power; that Hell should be able to *veto* Heaven . . . It must be one way or the other. Either the day must come when joy prevails and all the makers of misery are no longer able to infect it; or else for ever and ever the making of misery can destroy in others the happiness they reject for themselves. I know it has a grand sound to say ye'll accept no salvation which leaves even one creature in the dark outside. But watch that sophistry or ye'll make a Dog in a Manger the tyrant of the universe.[11]

With this discussion of hell we may seem to have wandered from the question, "What must God be like?" In fact, this discussion is essential to the answer. God is love. We must start with these words of St. John, "the disciple Jesus loved." But the love that is God is not indulgent, it makes demands on us. We are God's children, not God's pets. As God's children we may be asked to take part in our Father's work, share with his only begotten Son the work of suffering to save our fellow humans. Having shared Christ's suffering, we shall share Christ's glory (a point St. Paul makes repeatedly).

For Lewis, God is the Creator who is to be loved for giving us our existence, and making us the gift of all existence. As Lewis says in *Letters to Malcolm,* "I have tried . . . to make every pleasure into a channel of adoration. I don't mean simply by giving thanks. One must of course give thanks but I mean something different. . . . Gratitude exclaims, very properly: 'How good of God to give me this'; Adoration says: 'What must be the quality of that Being whose far-off and momentary coruscations are like this!' One's mind runs back up the sunbeam to the sun."[12]

Secondly, God is our Redeemer: "God so loved the world that he sent his only begotten Son to die for our sins." The point of the doctrine of Christ's divinity is that it is *God* who becomes man and dies for our sins, not some chosen human representative. The concept of a God who so loves us as to become human and be tortured to death for us surely is the most tremendous of the religious beliefs of humankind. If it were a fiction, it would be the high point of human imagination; if a fact, it is the most important fact there is.

The traditional Christian doctrine of the Trinity—that Father, Son, and Holy Spirit are equally God—is now so often misunderstood that it is worthwhile spending some time on Lewis's discussion of it. In *Mere Christianity,* Lewis points out that many people "feel that the mysterious something which is beyond all other things must be more than a person. Now the Christians quite agree. But the Christians are the only people who offer any idea of what a being that is beyond personality could be like. All the other people, though they say God is beyond personality, really think of Him as something less than personal. If you are looking for something superpersonal, something more than a person, then it is not a question of choosing between the Christian idea and the other ideas. The Christian idea is the only one on the market."[13]

What is "the Christian idea"? We said earlier that persons by nature have knowledge and will. The Three Persons in God share the same nature. They all have the same omniscient knowledge, they all share the same omnipotent and perfect will. It is impossible for one to know something that the others do not, or to will something that the others do not.

But a person is not just knowledge and will. I *have* knowledge and I *make* choices, but it is *I* who knows and wills. There are Three Persons who share the divine nature. How can they be distinguished? The traditional answer is "by their relation to each other." The Son eternally "proceeds" from the Father, the Holy Spirit eternally "proceeds" from both Father and Son. This relation of "proceeding from" is mysterious; it does not mean priority in time, it does not mean priority in dignity. The Christian creeds emphasize that Son and Holy Spirit are equally God, equally to be honored with the Father. Philosophers and logicians can point out that to distinguish three things purely by their relation to each other can be done only by a one-directional relation, holding in just the way that the "proceeding" relation is said to hold traditionally. A diagram here may be worth many words:

The three dots are uniquely describable: one has two arrows "going out" and none "coming in," one has one arrow "out" and one "in," and one dot has two arrows "in" and none "out." If any arrows were double-headed or if any were missing, or if any other arrangement of arrows were made, the three dots could not be uniquely distinguished *purely by their relation to each other*. In a diagram like this:

we can speak of the top dot, the left-bottom, and the right-bottom dots, but that brings in their relation to the observer and to the page. In the second diagram, the dots cannot be distinguished by their relation to *each other*. However, the Three Persons in God cannot be distinguished by anything outside of God—because it must be possible for God to exist whether or not anything else exists.

Although Lewis did not use this particular illustration or say a great deal about the relation between the Three Persons, he did explain how three persons can make up one God in an excellent teaching analogy found in "Beyond Personality." Does it seem strange to you that three persons can make up one God? he asked. You know that six squares can together make up one three-dimensional cube. If you remove any square, you no longer have a cube; but in three dimensions a square cannot exist alone as a zero-thickness object: it must be a surface of some three-dimensional object. While Lewis's interdependence analogy is not perfect, it is one of the best simple analogies for the Trinity ever given.

Lewis was even more concerned with the practical effect of the doctrine of the Trinity. If there are three persons in God, we can begin to see the full force of the idea that God is love. The life of God is a life of love between Father, Son, and Holy Spirit. *Our destiny is to be drawn into this life of love, and this brings out the third aspect of God as our Sanctifier: a parent who is making us, the adopted children of God, more and more into images of God. And what is it to be an image of God? It is to be a person whose life is to love: to love God, the supremely worthy object of love; to love our fellow humans as ourselves (and that includes the right kind of love for ourselves); and to love all the good things God has created for us. As St. John put it in 1 John 4:16–18, "God is love: he who dwells in love dwells in God, and God in him. That our life in the world should be like his means that His love has had its way with us to the full."*

Or as Lewis said in *Mere Christianity:*

And now what does it matter? It matters more than anything else in the world. The whole dance or drama or pattern of this three-Personal life is to be played out in each of us: or, putting it the other way around, each one of us has got to enter that pattern, take his place in that dance. There is no other way to happiness for which we were made. Good things as well as bad, you know, are caught by a kind of infection. If you want to get warm you must stand near the fire; if you want to get wet you must get into the water. If you want joy, power, peace, eternal life you must get close to, or even into the thing that has them. They are not a sort of prize which God could, if he chose, just hand out to anyone. They are a great fountain of energy and beauty spurting up at the very center of reality. If you are close to it the spray will wet you; if you are not, you will remain dry. Once a man is united to God how could he not live forever? Once a man is separated from God, what can he do but wither and die?[14]

4. Who Is Christ?

Who is Jesus Christ? Merely a very good man? A man with flaws and limitations, as some have claimed? A being greater than human but less than God? A mere mask or appearance of God? Or is Jesus Christ completely God and at the same time completely human, as traditional Christianity claims? Lewis took his stand on the traditional answer, claiming that all other answers could be shown to be unsatisfactory. Especially he rejected the notion, popular among "liberal" Christians and "reverent agnostics," that Christ was merely a great human teacher, a good man but no more. "He did not leave us that option," wrote Lewis in *Mere Christianity,* "he did not intend to."[1]

The question of what claims Christ made and how far we can trust these claims is very much mixed up with another question: how reliable are New Testament accounts? That, in turn, involves yet another problem: how believable are the accounts of miraculous events? Instead of artificially separating these questions, we will discuss them together in this chapter and the next, letting one question lead into another.

Let us begin where Lewis himself often began, with an argument that might be summarized as follows: Christ claimed to be God. He was either telling the truth, or he was insane, or he was a liar. Christ was not insane. He was not a liar. Therefore, his claims must be the truth. This argument leads us directly to the question of the authenticity of the New Testament. Even granted that in the New Testament as we now have it there are claims to divinity by Christ and on behalf of Christ—and some would dispute even this—could not these claims be later interpolations into a generally reliable historical record, or could not the whole New Testament be fictional or mythological?

That leads us directly into the third question, for the strongest reason for denying the historicity of the New Testament is the presence in it of accounts of miraculous events—events that seem to run contrary to our experience of the way the world operates. Surely, those accounts in themselves are enough to brand the New Testament as fairy tale or myth.

Let us begin with the first question: what claims did Christ make? Lewis typically began with something that Christ did repeatedly: he told people that their sins were forgiven. Take one striking incident recounted in Mark 2:12: Jesus was preaching to a large crowd inside a house. A paralyzed man was brought by some friends, who could not get through the crowd. In order to reach Jesus, his friends climbed onto the roof, removed some of the roof tiles, and lowered the man to the spot where Jesus stood preaching. Since entering a house in this way was a common technique of burglars, it has been suggested that the cripple and his friends might have been burglars, and the man might even have been paralyzed by an injury in some such burglary—perhaps a rope broke or the man fell from a roof.

Jesus' immediate reaction on seeing the man lowered from the roof to his feet was to say, "My son, your sins are forgiven." As Lewis pointed out, we are so used to such incidents in the New Testament that we do not see how extraordinary they are. Lewis wrote, "Moderns do not seem startled, as contemporaries were, by the claim Jesus there makes to forgive sins: not sins against Himself, just sins. Yet, surely if they actually met it, they would feel differently. Suppose [someone] told me that two of his colleagues had lost him a professorship by telling lies about his character and I replied, 'I forgive them both,' would he not think this an impertinence (both in the old and modern sense) bordering on insanity?"[2]

Lewis was especially fond of this example, because it is clear that such incidents of Jesus claiming to forgive sins cannot possibly be separated from the New Testament record. All of the Gospels, Lewis goes on to say, tell us the story of Jesus condemned to death by the Jews because they saw as blasphemous his claim to be the son of God: "Because you, who are only a man, are making yourself out to be God" (John 10:33). If this was a misunderstanding or misinterpretation, it is one that a good man would have been very much concerned to set straight: but there is no record of Jesus doing so. As Lewis wrote:

Then there is a curious thing which seems to slip out almost by accident. On one occasion this Man is sitting looking down on Jerusalem from the hill above it and suddenly in comes an extraordinary remark—"I keep on sending you prophets and wise men." Nobody comments on it. And yet, quite suddenly, almost incidentally, He is claiming to be the power that all through the centuries is sending wise men and leaders into the world. Here is another curious remark: in almost every religion there are unpleasant observances like fasting. This Man suddenly remarks one day, "No one need fast while I am here." Who is this Man who remarks that His mere presence suspends all normal rules? Who is the person who can suddenly tell the School they can have a half-holiday? Sometimes the statements put forward the assumption that He, the Speaker, is completely without sin or fault. This is always the attitude. "You, to whom I am talking, are all sinners," and He never remotely suggests that this same reproach can be brought against Him. He says again, "I am begotten of the One God, before Abraham was, I am," and remember what the words "I am" were in Hebrew. They were the name of God, which must not be spoken by any human being, the name which it was death to utter.[3]

The whole of Jesus' behavior as recounted in all four Gospels is inexplicable if Jesus did not claim to be God. Who but God could alter the law of God? ("You have heard that it was said to the people in the old days, 'You shall not murder. . . .' But I say to you anyone who is angry with his brother must stand his trial . . ." [Matt. 5:21–22].) Who but God would heal in his own name, not calling upon or praying to God? ("Then a leper came to Jesus. . . . 'If you want to, you can make me clean.' Jesus was filled with pity. . . . 'Of course I want to—be clean!' " [Matt. 8:1–3].)

When a close friend of Lewis's defended the view that Christ was not God, Lewis wrote back:

In Matt. 28:19 you already get the baptismal formula "In the name of the Father, the Son, the Holy Ghost." Who is this "Son"? Is the Holy Ghost a man? If not, does a man "send" Him (see John 15:26)? In Col. 1:12 Christ is "before all things and by Him all things consist." What sort of a man is this? I leave out the obvious place at the beginning of St. John's gospel. Take something much less obvious: When He weeps over Jerusalem (Matt. 23) why does He suddenly say (v. 34), "I send unto you prophets and wise men." *Who* could say this except either God or a lunatic? Who is this man who goes about forgiving sins? Or what about Mark 2:18–19. What *man* can announce that simply because he is present acts of penitence, such as fasting, are "off." Who can give the school a half-holiday except the Headmaster? The doctrine of Christ's divinity seems to me not something stuck on which you can unstick but something that peeps out at every point so that you'd have to unravel the whole web to get rid of it.[4]

As Lewis pointed out in *Mere Christianity* and elsewhere, the greater the goodness of a mere human, the less that person is inclined to claim divinity. All the great Jewish prophets, a line that culminated in St. John the Baptist, were careful to make clear that they rebuked and commanded in the name of the Lord, not in their own names. The great philosophers who turned the intellects of human beings toward things higher than themselves were all very clear about their own limited place in the scheme of things. Only in the case of Christ do we get what would be insanity or towering arrogance—if the claim were not true. As Lewis said:

On the one side, clear, definite moral teaching. On the other claims which, if not true, are those of a megalomaniac compared with whom Hitler was the most sane and humble of men. There is no half-way house and no parallel in other religions. If you had gone to Buddha and asked him, "Are you the son of Bramah?" he would have said, "My son, you are still in the vale of illusion." If you had gone to Socrates and asked, "Are you Zeus?" he would have laughed at you. . . . The idea of a great moral teacher saying what Christ said is out of the question. In my opinion the only person who can say that sort of thing is either God or a complete lunatic suffering from that form of delusion which undermines the whole mind of man. . . .[5]

In summary, Lewis asks "whether any hypothesis covers the facts so well as the Christian hypothesis . . . that God has come down into the created universe."[6]

As modern knowledge and understanding of traditional theology is so limited, it is worthwhile saying clearly just what it means to say that Jesus is God. The traditional doctrine is that the second person of the Trinity, the Son who "proceeds from the Father before all ages," took a human nature. This Person has, as God, divine omniscience and omnipotence. As man, he has a human will that must be submitted to the divine will, and human knowledge that is necessarily limited by human capacities. He has a human body that grows tired and hungry and can suffer pain. But the consciousness that has this weariness and hunger and pain is the consciousness of God the Son. The Person who is Jesus Christ is *completely* God and *completely* human: one *person* with two *natures*.

Why is the divinity of Christ so important? Why can we not simply say that whatever Christ is, he is worthy of our highest admiration and devotion? The answer is that the divinity of Christ is vital for our understanding of the notions of Redemption and Atonement. If Christ was merely a very good man, or even a being more than human but less than God, then the price for sin has been borne by someone other than God, and we are left with the idea of a God who demands punishment and is willing to punish an innocent person as a substitute for those who are guilty. On the other hand, the traditional Christian view says it was *God* who paid the price, *God* who took human nature to suffer and die to atone for sin; God the Son, the Second Person of the Trinity, not God the Father *or* God the Holy Spirit, but still *God.*

What is it to pay the price of sin, and why *must* it be paid? In *Mere Christianity,* Lewis begins to explain this by distinguishing the revealed fact from theories about the fact:

The central Christian belief is that Christ's death has somehow put us right with God and given us a fresh start. A good many theories have been held as to how it works; what all Christians are agreed on is that it does work. . . . Theories about Christ's death are not Christianity: they are explanations about how it works.[7]

Lewis goes on to discuss some theories about Christ's redemption of the human race. The first is what we may call the "debt" theory: human sin has created a debt that must be paid, and God incarnate in Christ has paid that debt for us. Indeed, some of the early Christian writers talk as if this debt was somehow owed to the Devil, who had a "mortgage" on human souls that was "paid off" by the voluntary sacrifice of Christ. Interestingly, this is the view of the Atonement that Lewis "transposed" into fiction in the first Narnia book, *The Lion, the Witch and the Wardrobe*. In the world of Narnia, the great lion Aslan plays the same part Christ plays in this world: he is the son of "the Great Emperor," the creator and ruler of Narnia. Four children from our world find their way to Narnia, and one of them, Edmund, betrays his brothers and sisters and goes over to the side of evil. His life is forfeited to the Witch, who plays the Devil's role in this Narnian tale, and she claims her right to Edmund's life. Aslan himself agrees to be killed in Edmund's place, to pay the price of Edmund's sin. Like Christ, Aslan suffers humiliation and death, and again like Christ, Aslan rises triumphantly from the dead.

It may well be that Lewis thought the simple act of substituting Aslan's death for Edmund's would be more understandable to children than the complicated idea of redemption. Children are not likely to worry about *why* the price had to be paid; as G. K. Chesterton noted, adults are sinners and like the idea of forgiveness, while children, who are innocent, love the idea of justice. Only a single passage in the Narnia books addresses this problem: one of the children suggests that Aslan somehow overthrow the law, or "Deep Magic," that gives the Witch the right to Edmund's blood.

"Work against the Emperor's magic?" said Aslan turning to her with something like a frown on his face. And nobody ever made that suggestion to him again.[8]

The idea conveyed is that Aslan respects his father's law—that even Aslan cannot simply *ignore* Edmund's guilt, free him from the rightful punishment by a mere act of power. Again, this is enough for children, but in the adult world we are likely, as Chesterton said, to prefer the idea of mercy, of forgiveness with no price attached. What is wrong with this idea?

Certainly we can point to some obvious facts. If something is genuinely and deeply wrong, like murder or torture or rape, it is rightly forbidden. If those who commit such acts are forgiven without any punishment, they are likely to take this forgiveness lightly and turn back easily to their sins. If they receive the full punishment due their sins, they may be embittered or rebellious. But suppose some innocent person were to voluntarily take their punishment for love of them? Would not all but the hardest hearts react to such an act by repentance and reformation?

This is certainly part of the story, and the whole of Christian literature resounds with the debt of gratitude we owe to Christ for suffering for us, and our obligation to repay this debt by the way we live our lives. For example, an old prayer attributed to St. Richard of Chichester, a medieval English bishop, goes as follows:

Thanks be to Thee, Lord Jesus Christ
For all the benefits Thou hast conferred upon us.
For all the pains and insults which Thou hast borne for us.
Oh, most merciful Redeemer, Friend and Brother,
   Let us know Thee more clearly
   Love Thee more dearly
   And follow Thee more nearly.

In *Mere Christianity,* Lewis emphasizes another aspect of Redemption. All of what we are able to do is in some sense a "participation" in the power of God. Our reason is a share of divine reason, our love a share of divine love, our creativity a share of divine creativity. But we need to repent, and in God there is no need for repentance. What is it to repent? To be separated from God, and by our own will to return to him. God became human, Lewis argues, to solve this problem:

We now need God's help in order to do something which God in His own nature never does at all—to surrender, to suffer, to submit, to die. Nothing in God's nature corresponds to this process at all. . . . But supposing that God became a man—suppose our human nature which can suffer and die was amalgamated with God's nature in one person— then that person could help us. He could surrender His will and die because He was man, and He could do it perfectly because He was God. You and I can go through this process only if God does it in us; but God can do it only because he becomes man. Our attempts at this dying will succeed only if we men share in God's dying, just as our thinking can succeed only because it is a drop out of the ocean of his intelligence: but we cannot share in God's dying unless God dies; and He cannot die except by being a man. That is the sense in which He pays our debt and suffers for us what He Himself need not suffer at all.[9]

In later life, Lewis felt that his understanding of Christ's Atonement was further illuminated by an idea he found in the teaching of his friend Charles Williams: the idea of "substitution," of one human being literally taking on and bearing the burdens of another. The fact that we can make sense of this, see it as a great and wonderful act of love when one human does it for another, helps us to see the "rightness" of God's love for us expressed in this way.

Toward the end of his life, when his wife was ill with a bone disease, Lewis experienced a possible instance of this "substitution" in his own life. His friend Nevill Coghill tells the story in passing, while discussing the influence of Williams on Lewis:

It was Charles Williams who expounded to him the doctrine of co-inherence and the idea that one had power to accept into one's own body the pain of someone else, through Christian love. This was a power which Lewis found himself later to possess, and which, he told me, he had been allowed to use to ease the suffering of his wife, a cancer victim, of whom the doctors had despaired. . . . He told me of having been allowed to accept her pain.

"You mean" (I said) "that her pain left her, and that you felt it for her in your body?"

"Yes," he said, "in my legs. It was crippling. But it relieved hers."[10]

At about the same time, Lewis wrote to another friend that Joy's bones were gaining calcium at the same rate that his were losing it, "a bargain (if it were one) for which I am heartily thankful."[11]

We are familiar with Christ's words in John 15:13, "Greater love has no man than this, that he lay down his life for his friend." They seem obviously true: love that sacrifices for the beloved is the highest form of love. But Christ's life gave us an ideal yet higher: "Greater love has no God than this, that He lay down His life for His creatures."

That non-Christians do not accept the divinity of Christ is of course to be expected: why would they be non-Christians if they accepted it? But some "liberal" Christians do not accept it either, and they are more concerned than non-Christians to try to argue that the New Testament does not actually teach this idea. Since arguments like Lewis's make it impossible for any clearheaded person to deny that the New Testament contains a claim to divinity by and for Christ, they attempt to preserve what they want of the New Testament and discard what they don't want, by saying that the parts they don't want are later interpolations into the historical record of Jesus' life and teaching.

Non-Christians, of course, don't usually bother with such contortions. Their attitude toward the New Testament is like their attitude toward, say, the Greek myths. "There is a good deal of nonsense here, mixed up with some truth. Discard the nonsense and preserve the truth: it doesn't matter much how they originally got mixed up." But "liberal" Christians want to have their cake and eat it too: keep the New Testament as a source of moral and religious authority, without accepting some parts of what it says.

The favored tactic for doing so goes something like this: "The original Jesus was a Jewish moral teacher with great goodness and great insight; his personality and teaching attracted many followers. When the 'Jesus Movement' spread outside of Judaism and made converts from the polytheistic Greek and Roman cultures, it was natural for these converts to think of Jesus in terms familiar to them—as a divine being, the son of a god. As accounts of Jesus' life and teaching were recorded, this sort of idea crept in and became part of the New Testament documents."

The first thing to realize is that this is a completely after-the-fact theory, based on no documentary evidence. We do not have early versions of the Gospels with no claims to divinity or accounts of miracles and later versions with those things added. What we have is a series of documents written at a time remarkably close to the events they relate—much closer than that of the ancient documents on which we base our accounts of history up until the last few centuries. Discovery of New Testament fragments, scientific dating, and textual as opposed to theoretical criticism, have driven the scientifically acknowledged date of the Gospels closer and closer to their traditional dates of composition, which were within the lifetime of multitudes of people who had known and heard Christ. The old theories about interpolation assumed that the process of interpolation in the texts occurred over a period of centuries; modern research has shown that there was simply not time for such a process to occur. In fact, we have almost the same dilemma with regard to the early church as we have with regard to Jesus: either the early Christian writers were liars, or they were deluded, or they recorded accurately what Jesus said and did. Now there is no question of interpolations gradually creeping in, century after century.

Lewis himself rarely got into the details of such controversies. His general approach was that he was not an expert on ancient languages, he was an expert on literature. The Gospels, supposed by some to be at least in part myth or legend, lack the characteristics of myth or legend: they don't satisfy human curiosity about things that myths and legends typically invent stories about; they insert odd little details which are just the sort of thing that would strike an eyewitness but that are not the sort of thing anyone would invent. "In one sense," Lewis says, "the Gospels aren't *good* enough to be myths." And he points out that:

The undermining of the old orthodoxy has been mainly the work of divines engaged in New Testament criticism. The authority of experts in that discipline is the authority in deference to whom we are asked to give up a huge mass of beliefs shared in common by the early Church, the Fathers, the Middle Ages, the Reformers, and the nineteenth century. I want to explain what it is that makes me sceptical about this authority. . . .

First then, whatever these men may be as Biblical critics, I distrust them as critics. They seem to me to lack literary judgment, to be imperceptive about the very quality of the texts they are reading. . . . If [someone] tells me something in a Gospel is legend or romance, I want to know how many legends or romances he has read, how well his palate is trained in detecting them by the flavour; not how many years he has spent on that Gospel. . . .

These men ask me to believe they can read between the lines of the old texts; the evidence is their obvious inability to read (in any sense worth discussing) the lines themselves. They claim to see fern-seed and can't see an elephant ten yards away in broad daylight.

Now for my second [point]. All theology of the liberal type involves at some point—and often involves throughout—the claim that the real behaviour and purpose and teaching of Christ came very rapidly to be misunderstood and misrepresented by his followers, and has been recovered or exhumed only by modern scholars. . . . The idea that any man or writer should be opaque to those who lived in the same culture, spoke the same language, shared the same habitual imagery and unconscious assumptions, and yet be transparent to those who have none of these advantages, is in my opinion preposterous. There is an *a priori* improbability in it which almost no argument and no evidence could counterbalance.

Thirdly, I find in these theologians a constant use of the principle that the miraculous does not occur . . . the rejection as unhistorical of all passages which narrate miracles is sensible if we start by knowing that the miraculous in general never occurs. . . . [But] this is a purely philosophical question. Scholars, as scholars, speak on it with no more authority than anyone else. The canon "If miraculous, unhistorical" is one they bring to their study of the texts, not one they have learned from it. If one is speaking of authority, the united authority of all the Biblical critics in the world counts here for nothing. On this they speak simply as men; men obviously influenced by, and perhaps insufficiently critical of, the spirit of the age they grew up in.[12]

Lewis's fourth point is that methods like those of the "demythologizers," when applied to his own work and that of his friends such as J. R. R. Tolkien, "[show] a record of 100 percent failure." Lewis concludes that the skepticism currently directed at the New Testament might better be applied to the methods and conclusions of the "demythologizers" themselves.

On the other hand, the traditional view of the Scripture which Lewis defends is that which has been held by most Christians in most ages. Some of the greatest intellects produced by the human race, men such as Augustine and Aquinas, Newton and Napier, Dante and Dr. Johnson, have found no intellectual difficulty in accepting it. The traditional view still has many defenders among biblical scholars, and it is not an answer to say that these are "conservative" scholars; they may hold the views on Scripture that they do because of their religious views, but they may equally well hold the religious views they do because they are convinced a certain view of Scripture is true. The change to modernistic views of Scripture is historically the result, not the cause, of changes in philosophy and theology.

If we stand back from the controversies and simply let the New Testament make its impact on us, we may be inclined to say with G. K. Chesterton, "The grinding power of the plain words of the Gospel story is like the power of mill-stones, and those who can read them simply enough will feel as if rocks had been rolled upon them. Criticism is only words about words, and of what use are words about such words as these?"[13]

5. Miracles and History

Lurking in the background of the discussion so far has been the question of miracles. The New Testament would be treated by the ordinary procedures of historical criticism if it did not contain accounts of miraculous events, and nothing as far-fetched as the demythologizer's theory of interpolation would ever have been accepted. But accounts of miraculous cures and other miraculous events are interwoven as tightly into the narrative as Christ's claims to divinity. Those who will not accept these accounts as historical must regard the Gospels as fabrications, in whole or in part. For those who wish to "salvage" the nonmiraculous parts of the New Testament account, the interpolation theory offers at least one possible explanation for the presence of miraculous elements.

It is important to realize that an interpolation theory accepted on such grounds is not based on the historical evidence at all: it is an after-the-fact theory that rejects accounts that purport to be historical not for historical reasons but for *philosophical* ones. If miracles do not happen, any account which contains miracles cannot be historical.

The problem does not arise in quite the same way for the Old Testament, for many parts of the Old Testament can be regarded as not intended to be history. As Lewis wrote to an inquirer:

I'm not a fundamentalist in the direct sense: one who starts out by saying, "Everything we read is literal fact." The presence of an allegorical or mystical element in *Genesis* was recognized by St. Jerome. Origen held *Job* to be a moral fable not a history. There is nothing new about such interpretation. But I often agree with the Fundamentalists about particular passages whose literal truth is rejected by many moderns. I reject nothing on the grounds of its being miraculous. I accept the story of the Fall, and I don't see what the findings of the scientists can say either for or against it. You can't see for looking at skulls and flint implements whether Man fell or not. But the question of the Fall seems to me quite independent of the question of evolution. I don't mind whether God made Man out of earth or whether "earth" merely means "previous material of some sort." If the deposits make it probable that man's physical ancestors "evolved," no matter. It leaves the essence of the Fall itself intact. Don't let us confuse physical development with spiritual."[1]

Lewis explored the problems involved more fully in *Reflections on the Psalms:*

The real reason why I can accept as historical a story in which a miracle occurs is that I have never found any philosophical grounds for the universal negative proposition that miracles do not happen. I have to decide on quite other grounds (if I decide at all) whether a given narrative is historical or not. The *Book of Job* appears to me unhistorical because it begins about a man quite unconnected with all history or even legend, with no genealogy, living in a country of which the Bible elsewhere has hardly anything to say; because, in fact, the author quite obviously writes as a story-teller not as a chronicler.

I have no difficulty in accepting, say, the view of those scholars who tell us that the account of Creation in *Genesis* is derived from earlier Semitic stories which were Pagan and mythical. . . . Something originally merely natural—the kind of myth that is found amongst most nations—will have been raised by God above itself, qualified by Him and compelled by Him to serve purposes which of itself it would not have served. Generalising thus, I take it that the whole Old Testament consists of the same sort of material as any other literature—chronicle (some of it obviously pretty accurate), poems, moral and political diatribes, romances, and what not; but all taken into the service of God's word.[2]

At any rate, as the problems raised by the Old Testament are too complex to go into here, we will confine our discussion of miracles to those recounted in the New Testament.

It is sometimes alleged that "experience" or "history" shows that miracles do not happen. But that argument commits the fallacy known as "begging the question"—that is, assuming what you are supposed to be proving. We are faced with what purport to be historical accounts of miraculous events. We cannot settle the question of whether these accounts are true by saying "history shows that miracles don't happen," because whether history shows that or not is the very question we are trying to answer. As Lewis points out in *Miracles:*

The ordinary procedure of the modern historian, even if he admits the possibility of miracle, is to admit no particular instance of it until every possibility of "natural" explanation has been tried and failed. That is, he will accept the most improbable "natural" explanations rather than say that a miracle occurred. Collective hallucination, hypnotism of unconsenting spectators, widespread instantaneous conspiracy in lying by persons not otherwise known to be liars and not likely to gain by the lie —all these are known to be very improbable events: so improbable that, except for the special purpose of excluding a miracle, they are never suggested. But they are preferred to the admission of a miracle.

Such a procedure is, from the purely historical point of view, sheer midsummer madness *unless* we start by knowing that any Miracle whatever is more improbable than the most improbably natural event. Do we know this? . . .

Ever since Hume's famous *Essay* it has been believed that historical statements about miracles are the most intrinsically improbable of all historical statements. According to Hume, probability rests on what may be called the majority vote of our past experiences. The more often a thing has been known to happen, the more probable it is that it should happen again; and the less often the less probable. Now the regularity of Nature's course, says Hume, is supported by something better than the majority vote of past experiences: it is supported by their unanimous vote, or, as Hume says, by "firm and unalterable experience." There is, in fact, "uniform experience" against Miracle; otherwise, says Hume, it would not be a miracle. A miracle is therefore the most improbable of all events. It is always more probable that the witnesses were lying or mistaken than that a miracle occurred.

Now of course we must agree with Hume that if there is absolutely "uniform experience" against miracles, if in other words they have never happened, why then they never have. Unfortunately we know the experience against them to be uniform only if we know that all the reports of them are false. And we can know all the reports to be false only if we know already that miracles have never occurred. In fact, we are arguing in a circle.[3]

Another argument often heard is that "science" shows that miracles *cannot* happen, that science gives us a picture of a universe ruled by laws. Miracles, as supposed violations of these laws, cannot occur. About this Lewis pointed out:

> But if we admit God, must we admit Miracle? Indeed, indeed, you have no security against it. That is the bargain. Theology says to you in effect, "Admit God and with Him the risk of a few miracles, and I in return will ratify your faith in uniformity as regards the overwhelming majority of events." The philosophy which forbids you to make uniformity absolute is also the philosophy which offers you solid grounds for believing it to be general, to be *almost* absolute. The Being who threatens Nature's claim to omnipotence confirms her in her lawful occasions. Give us this ha'porth of tar and we will save the ship. The alternative is really much worse. Try to make Nature absolute and you find that her uniformity is not even probable. By claiming too much, you get nothing. You get the deadlock, as in Hume. Theology offers you a working arrangement, which leaves the scientist free to continue his experiments and the Christian to continue his prayers.[4]

Lewis objected to defining miracles as *violations* of natural law. He thought of them as interventions in the normal course of nature by a higher power outside of nature. Notice that by Lewis's definition, no event that occurs as part of the natural order of things, no matter how improbable or how faith-inspiring, will count as a miracle. There may be a wider and looser sense of miracle in which striking coincidences that inspire religious belief are called "miracles," but they are not miracles in the stricter and narrower sense Lewis uses.

Before we can speak of exceptions to the natural order of things, we must believe that there *is* a natural order of things. To a person who believes there is no natural order, that the universe is chaotic, that its apparent order and understandability is an illusion, the idea of miracle holds no meaning, for that idea depends on contrast. Exceptions to rules or patterns require the existence of rules or patterns for them to be exceptions to. Science gives us an enormously strong argument against the idea that the universe is chaotic and without order and pattern, and if anyone really wished to challenge this we would have to settle that issue before arguing about miracles. But if the natural order is the result of God's action, sometimes God's actions might make exceptions to the natural order. Such an exception would be like the exceptions to established rules and procedures that we sometimes make—for example, allowing a particularly gifted child to skip grades, or declaring a holiday on a normal work day. Of course, exceptions must be rare if rules are to be relied on, but we can live perfectly well with occasional exceptions to a system of rules or procedures. We may or may not think Gerald Ford's pardon of expresident Nixon wise or fair, but occasional exceptions to legal procedures, such as presidential pardon, do not make our legal system chaotic or unreliable.

Furthermore, provided that God wishes to give us strong evidence that a given message has His authority behind it, there would seem to be no better way than through miracles. If I claim to have authority in an organization, my ability to suspend the rules or make exception to usual procedures would give strong evidence of my authority. You might meditate on the problem of how a God who never interfered with the working of the universe could establish his message as authoritative.

The scientist, of course, *as* a scientist, must ignore the possibility of miracles, just as the lawyer, *as* a lawyer, must ignore the possibility of a presidential pardon for his client, since there is nothing he or she can do *as a lawyer* which will ensure such a pardon. A pardon is a free action by the President, which cannot be guaranteed by any legal maneuver. Similarly, a miracle is a free act by God which the scientist cannot bring within *his* procedures.

A presidential pardon is like a miracle in that, once granted, it has legal consequences, although its *origin* is outside ordinary legal procedures. A miracle, once it has occurred, has consequences that fit into the kind of patterns scientists study: drinking too much of the wine Christ made from water at Cana in Galilee would have made a wedding guest drunk, and if a scientist had been there with instruments he or she could have verified, though not explained, the change and measured the alcoholic content of the wine made from water.

It is important to note that a presidential pardon does not violate any laws, nor does it suspend the laws in the sense that at a given time or place some laws cease to operate in all cases as if, for example, the laws of libel were suspended in Hannibal, Missouri, on the first Sunday in March, so that no libels in that place or time were punishable. Rather, an individual exception is made to the law, so that of two men convicted of the same crime at the same time, one may be pardoned and the other not. Similarly, a miracle does not *violate* the laws of nature, nor suspend them for all events at a given time or place: the water in one jar might be changed to wine, and that in an adjacent jar be unchanged. Lazarus may be raised and a man in an adjacent tomb who died at the same time may remain dead.

A presidential pardon cannot be compelled by any legal means, it can only be asked for. It is a free act of the president. Similarly, a miracle cannot be brought about by scientific means, it can only be prayed for. It is a free act of God. A presidential pardon cannot be predicted from the legal facts, and it creates no precedent: a pardon may be granted in one case, and in precisely similar circumstances another request may be denied. Similarly, a miracle cannot be predicted by scientific means, and gives no scientific grounds for prediction once it has occurred: the miracle at Cana does not increase the probability that water will change to wine in similar circumstances. Scientists, as such, have no concern with miracles, for they cannot predict them, bring them about, or draw from them any conclusions about the future course of nature. A miracle is supernatural, and therefore of no scientific interest.

We could not settle whether presidential pardons are possible by looking at the day-to-day business of the courts; rather, we must ask the kind of legal system we live under. Likewise, we cannot settle whether miracles occur by looking at the ordinary course of nature; we must ask what kind of universe we live in. This is a philosophical, not a scientific question. One relevant philosophical consideration in determining whether miracles are possible is that a universe made by God leaves room for confidence in human reason, whereas a universe of natural necessity does not, as was argued in Chapter 2.

If we conclude that miracles are possible, we must consider them as one possible explanation for certain events recorded in history. Early Christians claimed that the tomb of Christ was empty and that Christ had risen from the dead. The Roman and Jewish authorities did not refute this claim by producing the body, as they certainly would have done had *they* removed it from the tomb. The Apostles suffered persecution, hardship, and martyrdom to proclaim the message of Christ risen from the dead, which they surely would not have done if *they* had removed and hidden Christ's body. No naturalistic explanation that tries to explain the disappearance of the body, and the confidence of the early Christians, comes anywhere near accounting for all the facts.

If miracles were impossible, we would have to try to account for the data in some other way; but there is no good argument which shows miracles are impossible. If miracles were tremendously improbable, many times more so than the most farfetched naturalistic explanation of the data, then it might be reasonable to accept an otherwise implausible naturalistic explanation. But there is no argument to show that miracles are tremendously improbable. It is not enough to say that they are rare and unusual, for rare and unusual events might still be expected in given circumstances. It is rare to have world records in athletic events broken, but it is to be expected at the Olympic Games. President Ford's pardon of ex-president Nixon was a rare and unusual event, but not unexpected in the very unusual circumstances which then prevailed. The Resurrection of Christ was a rare and unusual event, but in the context of his life and teaching, was it unexpected?

Rare and unusual as miracles are, it is possible to give a general idea of the circumstances in which they may be expected. The first is extraordinary goodness or holiness on the part of the miracle worker. As the man born blind said to the Jews, "We know for certain that God does not answer the prayers of sinners" (John 9:31). The second circumstance is the need to authenticate a message from God. Christ was as good and holy the year before he began his public ministry as he was after he began it, but he did not begin to work miracles until he began to preach. There is, I think, a third condition: a minimal openness and willingness to learn on the part of the audience. In some places Christ worked few miracles because of the hardness of heart found in those places. Christ worked no miracles at Herod's request; he cast none of his pearls before that swine.

When we apply this to ourselves, says Lewis:

You are probably quite right in thinking that you will never see a miracle done: you are probably equally right in thinking that there was a natural explanation of anything in your past life which seemed, at the first glance, to be "rum" or "odd." God does not shake miracles into Nature at random as if from a pepper-caster. They come on great occasions: they are found at the great ganglions of history—not of political or social history, but of that spiritual history which cannot be fully known by men. If your own life does not happen to be near one of those great ganglions, how should you expect to see one? If we were heroic missionaries, apostles, or martyrs, it would be a different matter. But why you or I? Unless you live near a railway, you will not see trains go past your windows. How likely is it that you or I will be present when a peace-treaty is signed, when a great scientific discovery is made, when a dictator commits suicide? That we should see a miracle is even less likely. Nor, if we understand, shall we be anxious to do so. "Nothing almost sees miracles but misery." Miracles and martyrdoms tend to bunch about the same areas of history—areas we have naturally no wish to frequent. Do not, I earnestly advise you, demand an ocular proof unless you are already certain that it is not forthcoming.[5]

Let us turn to the related question of what miracles prove. If it is granted, at least for the sake of argument, that God exists, that miracles are possible, and that we have good historical evidence that miracles marked the beginning of Christianity, does this prove the Christian claim to the truth of the revelation given to us by Christ? To establish this, we will have to counter three apparent difficulties.

The first difficulty is what we might call the problem of "contradictory" miracles. If it were the case that genuine miracles were worked in support of contradictory religious revelations, we would not know what to think—it would be as if a witness whose integrity we were absolutely sure of gave contradictory testimony for both sides of a dispute. Something would have to give. We would have to think the witness was not really honest, or deny that he actually gave the testimony on both sides, or find some way of showing that the contradiction was only apparent.

Similarly, if it is claimed that miracles are worked in support of contradictory religious revelations, we would have to give up the idea of miracles as proving a system of religion unless we could show that the contradiction was only apparent, or that one set of opposed miracles was not genuine.

In some cases, I think we can show that there is no genuine conflict. I accept both Old Testament and New Testament miracles, but I would deny the claim, made by some, that the Old Testament miracles worked in the name of the One God of Judaism are in some ways incompatible with New Testament miracles worked in the name of God the Father, God the Son, and God the Holy Spirit. (This is, of course, because I would deny, on theological grounds, that Christian trinitarianism amounts to tritheism.)

More broadly, Lewis did not believe that the Christian needs to deny the possibility that God might have worked miracles for the "virtuous pagans" before Christ, to encourage them to emphasize those parts of their religion closest to the truth. If, for instance, God had worked a miracle for the Egyptian Pharaoh Amenhotep in support of his efforts to establish monotheism and overthrow the dark gods of old Egypt, this would be no challenge to Christianity, even though Amenhotep's monotheism might have been very crude and contained elements of untruth. In *Miracles,* Lewis says of this kind of case:

> I do not think that it is the duty of a Christian apologist (as many sceptics suppose) to disprove all stories of the miraculous which fall outside the Christian records, nor of a Christian man to disbelieve them. I am in no way committed to the assertion that God has never worked miracles through and for Pagans or never permitted created supernatural beings to do so. If, as Tacitus, Suetonius, and Dion Cassius relate, Vespasian performed two cures, and if modern doctors tell me that they could not have been performed without miracle, I have no objection. But I claim that the Christian miracles have a much greater intrinsic probability in virtue of their organic connection with one another and with the whole structure of the religion they exhibit. If it can be shown that one particular Roman emperor—and, let us admit, a fairly good emperor as emperors go—was once empowered to do a miracle, we must of course put up with the fact. But it would remain a quite isolated and anomalous fact. Nothing comes of it, nothing leads up to it, it establishes no body of doctrine, explains nothing, is connected with nothing. And this, after all, is an unusually favorable instance of a non-Christian miracle. The immoral and sometimes almost idiotic interferences attributed to gods in Pagan stories, even if they had a trace of historical evidence, could be accepted only on the condition of our accepting a wholly meaningless universe. What raises infinite difficulties and solves none will be believed by a rational man only under absolute compulsion.[6]

The truth of Christianity would only be threatened by genuine miracles worked in opposition to Christian claims or in support of incompatible claims. If, for instance, a Moslem holy man raised a man from the dead in order to persuade Christians that Mohammed's revelation had superseded that of Christ, this would be a case of genuine incompatibility. However, so far from any case of this kind being established, I believe that no case of this kind has ever been claimed. General statements are often made by opponents of Christianity that miracles are claimed by all religions, but established cases of these alleged claims are hard to come by.

About alleged miracles in Buddhism, Lewis had this to say:

Sometimes the credibility of the miracles is in an inverse ratio to the credibility of the religion. Thus miracles are (in late documents, I believe) recorded of the Buddha. But what could be more absurd than that he who came to teach us that Nature is an illusion from which we must escape should occupy himself in producing effects on the Natural level —that he who comes to wake us from a nightmare should *add* to that nightmare? The more we respect his teaching the less we could accept his miracles. But in Christianity, the more we understand what God it is who is said to be present and the purpose for which He is said to have appeared, the more credible the miracles become. That is why we seldom find the Christian miracles denied except by those who have abandoned some part of the Christian doctrine.[7]

The second major difficulty regarding the evidential value of miracles is the objection to miracles on the grounds that what seems to us to be an exception to the natural order may merely be the operation of some natural regularities that we do not yet understand. Perhaps, continues this argument, Jesus was merely a rare type of charismatic personality who could arouse such faith in people that their minds acted on their bodies in a way that freed them from illness. After all, the relation between mind and body is mysterious, and some studies suggest that mental attitude has a great deal to do with illness. Thus, someday we may understand scientifically, and even be able to reproduce, some of Christ's apparently miraculous cures.

This is an extremely weak argument, like any that depends on what science *may* be able to discover in the future. What range of illnesses and cures is this theory supposed to account for? Perhaps, for example, when Christ cured a paralytic the paralysis was hysterical and hence subject to psychosomatic healing. But what about Christ's cure of leprosy? What about his cure of the man blind since birth? It is no use saying that psychosomatic illnesses cured by the impact of a charismatic personality account for *some* of Christ's cures and that the rest are fictional, for this would be blatant picking and choosing among the evidence. If I am allowed to pick which of the evidence I will explain, and reject the rest, I can make almost any theory look plausible.

About healing miracles, Lewis said:

> The miracles of *Healing,* to which I turn next, are now in a peculiar position. Men are ready to admit that many of them happened, but are inclined to deny that they were miraculous. The symptoms of very many diseases can be aped by hysteria, and hysteria can often be cured by "suggestion." It could, no doubt, be argued that such suggestion is a spiritual power, and therefore (if you like) a supernatural power, and that all instances of "faith healing" are therefore miracles. But in our terminology they would be miraculous only in the same sense in which every instance of human reason is miraculous: and what we are now looking for is miracles other than that. My own view is that it would be unreasonable to ask a person who has not yet embraced Christianity in its entirety to allow that all the healings mentioned in the Gospels were miracles—that is, that they go beyond the possibilities of human "suggestion." It is for the doctors to decide as regards each particular case —supposing that the narratives are sufficiently detailed to allow even probable diagnosis. . . . So far from belief in miracles depending upon ignorance of natural law, we are here finding for ourselves that ignorance of law makes miracle unascertainable.[8]

Of course, the decisive cases against any theory of psychosomatic cures are the raisings from the dead reported in all four Gospels. A last-ditch attempt to explain these "naturally" might be to allege that the seemingly dead persons were only in a cataleptic state; but as cases of this kind are so rare, to allege this as an explanation of the raising of the daughter of the Jairus, *and* the son of the widow of Naim, *and* Lazarus, involves coincidence to a fantastic degree. Each of these accounts is highly circumstantial, and none can be plausibly treated as a variation on one of the others.

In other words, proponents of the view that Christ's cures were psychosomatic—"faith healings" in a limiting sense—must decide whether they accept the written records as factual or fictional, or believe them to be a mixture of both. If the records are fictional, the cures need not be explained. If factual, all the reported miracles must be accounted for, not just those that can be plausibly explained on naturalistic grounds. If it is alleged that there is a mixture of fact and fiction, some independent standard must be used to judge what is factual and what is fictional. We cannot in logic allow the principle of choice, "What I can explain is fact, the rest is fiction."

Those who say that even raisings from the dead can be accounted for by yet-unknown natural laws must explain a tremendous implausibility: either that these laws operated coincidentally around Jesus, or that an obscure provincial carpenter somehow was able to discover and use natural powers that none of the sages had been able to master or control.

A final difficulty concerning the evidential value of miracles rests on the fear of some that a supernatural power other than God might account for the wonders worked by Christ—that Jesus did his works, if not by the power of Beelzebub, then at least by the power of some spiritual being less than God. To say what power this might be, of course, one would have to give a theological account of the existence of powers greater than human, and how each is related to the other.

Consider, however, a line of argument sometimes heard from people influenced by some Eastern religions, which goes something like this: "Yes, of course Jesus was able to do apparently miraculous things; He was a Master or Adept, and they can all do things of this sort. Jesus, living where and when he did, tried to teach the Palestinian peoples a simple religion of love, put in terms of their own religious concepts; and this message has reached us in a distorted form. His real power lay in spiritual enlightenment, which you can learn by practicing yoga (or going to Tibet, or studying with Mahatma X, or the like)."

This again is a large blank check, now drawn not on science but on some form of mystical religion. A friend of mine, arguing religion with opponents who seemed dogmatically sure of what God could or could not create, challenged them, who claimed to know so much of creation, to create just one small rabbit—"to establish confidence." A similar challenge might be put to the exponents of Eastern wisdom: to duplicate even the least of Christ's miracles to establish their claims. If they admit their own lack of power but claim others have performed some feats as great as Christ's, the problem simply reduces to the problem of evidence for rival miracles discussed earlier.

Acceptance of miracles performed by some other supernatural power raises a theological question: whether a wise and loving God would allow people to be misled by permitting some lesser being to work apparent miracles. Real raising from the dead, creation of genuine food or wine—such miracles seem by nature to be God's province only. But even if such things as mind-reading or the manipulation of matter in scientifically inexplicable ways could be done by lesser powers than God, would God permit such occurrences in a context that would give rise to a false belief in men of goodwill, or seriously challenge the true beliefs of those who are on the right path? A priori, it would seem not; and there is no reliable record of any such occurrences. (This is not to say that God may not sometimes permit "wonders" to be worked in order to refute them by his own power, as shown in the story of the girl with the "prophetic spirit" in Acts 16:16–20.)

The preceding comments give some indication of the lines along which the evidential value of miracles must be assessed. Are there indeed rival miracles? Can miracles be attributable to lesser powers than God? If the answer to all these questions is "no," we are forced to grant that the finger of God is among us, and ask in which way that finger points.

It would be easy to say that Christ's miracles point to the truth of his message, leaving it to theologians to argue what that message is. Whatever theologians may say, however, one point should be clear. If we admit the full reality of Christ's miracles on the grounds we have discussed, our inescapable conclusion must be the divinity of Christ, in a full sense: Christ as God the Son, coequal and coeternal with the Father. The Old Testament prophets worked their wonders in the name of God, imploring God, invoking his name. But Christ worked miracles and forgave sins with his own power, and his followers worked miracles and forgave sins in his name: "Gold and silver have I none; what I have I give to you. In the name of Jesus Christ of Nazareth rise up and walk" (Acts 3:6–7). No great servant of God has healed or forgiven in his own name except Christ—who was not a servant but the Master come to serve.

6. Faith and Reason

To some believers, a good deal of the argumentation in the preceding chapters will seem beside the point. "Religion," they will say, "is a matter of faith, not of argument." They assume that faith and argument are mutually exclusive, that faith can be defined (as one unfriendly critic defined it) as "believing without regard to the evidence," or even "believing contrary to the evidence" (perhaps this is what the critic really meant). For any real understanding of C. S. Lewis, it is important to realize that, for him, faith and reason were definitely *not* opposed. He thought faith should be based on the evidence, not fly in the face of the evidence. To explain and defend Lewis's views on this point, we shall have to make the following distinctions between: (1) Our act of accepting a religious belief; (2) the way we hold that belief; (3) maintaining that belief in the face of difficulties; and (4) living up to our commitment to that belief.

These distinctions can be applied to cases other than those of religious belief. Consider a man who comes to believe that smoking is dangerous to his health. We can ask: (1) How and why the man accepted this belief; (2) how strongly he holds that belief; (3) whether he is able to maintain this belief in the face of his cravings; and (4) whether his behavior is consistent with the belief.

With regard to the first question, Lewis maintained that the great majority of religious believers throughout the ages have held their beliefs on the basis of what they judge to be good evidence:

[The] man who accepts Christianity always thinks he has good evidence whether like Dante *fisici e metafisici argomenti,* * or historical evidence, or the evidence of religious experience, or authority or all these together. For of course authority, however we may value it in this or that particular instance, is a kind of evidence. All of our historical beliefs, many of our beliefs about matters that concern us in everyday life, are accepted on the authority of other human beings, whether we are Christians, Atheists, Scientists or Men-in-the-Street.[1]

Concerning the strength with which religious beliefs should be held, Lewis said:

[A] special usage [of "belief"] is "I believe" as uttered by a Christian. There is no great difficulty in making the hardened materialist understand, however little he approves, the sort of central attitude which this "I believe" expresses. The materialist need only picture himself replying to some report of a miracle "I don't believe it" and then imagine this same degree of belief on the opposite side. He knows that he cannot then and there produce a refutation of the miracle which would have the certainty of mathematical proof; but the formal possibility that the miracle might after all have occurred does not really trouble him any more than a fear that water might not be H and O. Similarly the Christian does not necessarily claim to have demonstrative proof, but the formal possibility that God does not exist is not necessarily present in the form of the least actual doubt. . . . Belief, in this sense, seems to me to be assent to a proposition which we think so overwhelmingly probable that there is a psychological exclusion of doubt, though not a logical exclusion of dispute. . . .[2]

As examples of nonreligious beliefs that we hold with this kind of certainty, Lewis cites "our belief in the reality of the eternal world and of other people—if you prefer it a disbelief in solipsism." Challenged by a clever skeptic to *prove* that other people besides ourselves exist, or that the apparently real world is not a dream, we might not be able to give a "demonstrative" proof, one "which would have the certainty of a mathematical demonstration" for our beliefs. But we have not the least *real* doubt on these points.

---

*I.e., "scientific and philosophical arguments."

Given this degree of certainty, it is quite appropriate to carefully examine contrary arguments. Remember, Lewis's definition of religious belief says there is "not a logical exclusion of dispute." Still, we do not approach such arguments with any expectation that our belief will be refuted, or any fear that it will.

What about the *"obstinacy* in belief," the "holding fast to faith" in the face of apparent difficulties that seems to be recommended by many Christian teachers? Lewis says:

> There is of course no question so far of belief without evidence. We must beware of confusion between the way in which a Christian first adheres to certain propositions and the way in which he afterwards adheres to them. These must be carefully distinguished. Of the second, it is true, in a sense, to say that Christians do recommend a certain discounting of apparent contrary evidence, and I will later attempt to explain why. But so far as I know it is not expected that a man should assent to these propositions in the first place without evidence or in the teeth of the evidence.[3]

What is Lewis's explanation of why Christians recommend "a certain discounting of apparent contrary evidence?" He gives it in terms of trust in or faithfulness to *persons:*

> We think we can see already why, if our original belief is true, such trust beyond the evidence, against much apparent evidence, has to be demanded of us. We believe [God's] intention is to create a certain personal relation between Himself and us, a relation really *sui generis* but analogically describable in terms of filial or of erotic love. Complete trust is an ingredient in that relation—such trust as could have no room to grow except where there is also room for doubt. . . . What would a moment before, have been variations of opinion, now becomes variations in your personal attitude to a Person. You are no longer faced with an argument which demands your assent, but with a Person who demands your confidence. . . .
>
> Our opponents, then, have a perfect right to dispute with us about the grounds of our original assent. But they must not accuse us of sheer insanity if, after the assent has been given, our adherence to it is no longer proportioned to every fluctuation of the apparent evidence. They cannot of course be expected to know on what our assurance feeds, and

how it revives and is always rising from its ashes. They cannot be expected to see how the *quality* of the object which we think we are beginning to know by acquaintance drives us to the view that if this were a delusion then we should have to say that the universe had produced no real thing of comparable value and that all explanations of the delusion seemed somehow less important than the thing explained. That is knowledge we cannot communicate. But they can see how the assent, of necessity, moves us from the logic of speculative thought into what might perhaps be called the logic of personal relations. What would, up till then, have been variations simply of opinion become variations of conduct by a person to a Person. *Credere Deum esse* turns into *Credere in Deum.* And *Deum* here is this God, the increasingly knowable Lord.[4]

So far, we have been talking about intellectual assent, and "belief" rather than "faith" seemed the appropriate term. But faith includes more than belief: it also includes commitment, which leads naturally to action. If I have faith in a presidential candidate, I will support him, perhaps work for his election, certainly vote for him if I can. If I have faith in God, I will try to do what God asks of me. As John says in 1 John 2:3–4, "The man who claims to know God but does not obey His laws is not only a liar but lives in self-delusion."

The sense in which faith is a virtue, something morally praiseworthy, varies with the aspect of faith we are speaking of. We can praise someone for assenting to the truth, as we might praise a judge or jury for reaching the right verdict in a difficult case. We can praise people for the strength of their faith, or for holding their convictions strongly, without timidity or vacillation. But, most often, we praise faith as a virtue when we think of it as persistence in belief despite obstacles, or commitment to belief which naturally leads to action. The obstacles to persistence in faith are more likely to be such things as external persecution or emotion-based doubts than they are to be arguments or apparent counterevidence. Thus the martyr—the man or woman who gives his or her life rather than deny the faith—is the prototypical Christian hero. And "temptations against faith" are usually things—such as apparently unjustified suffering—of which we were intellectually aware, but which are brought home to us emotionally by personal experience.

When Lewis's beloved wife died painfully of cancer, Lewis knew intellectually the Christian answer to the "problem of pain," but emotionally he felt that God was cruel or unjust—feelings he expressed with painful honesty in *A Grief Observed.* This is precisely what is usually meant by a "temptation against faith"—a powerful emotional pull against our intellectual convictions. In *Mere Christianity,* Lewis uses the analogy of being on a hike and trusting a map that shows the destination as only a few miles from the landmark passed a while back, although the hiker feels as if he had walked *twenty* miles since then. In his novel *Perelandra,* Lewis gives vivid fictional form to this type of situation. While walking at night from a railroad station to a friend's cottage, Lewis (who appears as a minor character in the novel) is bombarded with doubts about his journey and his friend, and is tempted to rationalize a decision to turn back. At one point, the doubts take the form of questioning his friend Ransom's honesty, and the fictional Lewis says:

> The reader, not knowing Ransom, will not understand how contrary to all reason this idea was. The rational part of my mind even at that moment knew perfectly well that even if the whole universe were crazy and hostile Ransom was sane and wholesome and honest. And this part of my mind in the end sent me forward—but with a reluctance and a difficulty I can hardly put into words.[5]

In theological terms, what the fictional Lewis has done is to overcome a temptation against his faith—not in God, but in his friend Ransom.

Lewis points out in *Mere Christianity* that many temptations against faith arise from impulses to disobey the moral law sanctioned by that faith, or from mere rebellion of our moods:

> I am not asking anyone to accept Christianity if his best reasoning tells him that the weight of the evidence is against it. That is not the point at which Faith comes in. But supposing a man's reason once decides that the weight of the evidence is for it. I can tell that man what is going to

happen to him in the next few weeks. There will come a moment when there is bad news, or he is in trouble, or is living among a lot of other people who do not believe it, and all at once his emotions will rise up and carry out a sort of blitz on his belief. Or else there will come a moment when he wants a woman, or wants to tell a lie, or feels very pleased with himself, or sees a chance of making a little money in some way that is not perfectly fair: some moment, in fact, at which it would be convenient if Christianity were not true. And once again his wishes and desires will carry out a blitz. I am not talking of moments at which any real new reasons against Christianity turn up. Those have to be faced and that is a different matter. I am talking about moments where a mere mood rises up against it.

Now faith, in the sense in which I am here using the word, is the art of holding on to things your reason has once accepted, in spite of your changing moods. For moods will change, whatever view your reason takes.[6]

At this point it seems fair to say that many of the common objections to faith have been answered. The objector says, "If faith and reason conflict, we should choose reason." Lewis answers, "They don't conflict." The objector says, "It is wrong to believe without regard to the evidence, or against the evidence." Lewis replies, "But that is not what Christians mean by faith." There remains a line of objection that says it is somehow wrong to make the kind of commitment faith requires. Sometimes this objection is prudential: we might be fooled or duped if we commit ourselves. But sometimes the view has an ethical basis: respect for "truth," or "the scientific method," or "rational inquiry," requires us to suspend judgment if any doubt remains, to always be open to new evidence and never to lock ourselves into any belief.

Against the prudential objection, Lewis argued that the nature of the personal relationship God is trying to establish with us precludes absolute guarantee: some room must be left for our freedom, our generosity. As Screwtape says to Wormwood, "The Irresistible and Indisputable are two weapons which the very nature of [God's] scheme forbids Him to use."[7]

The "ethical" objection to a commitment of faith assumes a great deal about values. If it is based on the idea that "truth" "science" or "reason" must override all other considerations, this seems to imply precisely the sort of unlimited commitment that is criticized in religion. The Christian, for whom truth is *one* of the names of God, can justify a commitment to truth and, at the same time, be certain it does not conflict with religious commitment. But it is not clear how a materialist is to justify any moral absolute, including the moral claims of truth, in whose name he or she criticizes religious faith.

I suspect that many opponents of Christianity will not recognize Lewis's "Christian rationalist" view of faith as being what *they* mean by faith. Many anti-Christian polemicists will be reluctant to relinquish the straw man of "irrational faith" that they have attacked for so long. A natural move for such people is to argue that, though a few sophisticated Christian intellectuals may accept Lewis's account of faith, for the great majority of Christians faith is merely a "leap in the dark," a commitment not based on evidence or argument.

In discussing criticism of this kind, Lewis first made a distinction between faith as intellectual assent (which he called "Faith-A"), and faith as commitment to God (which he called "Faith-B"):

[These] arguments for the existence of God are presumably intended to produce Faith-A. No doubt those who construct them are anxious to produce Faith-A because it is a necessary condition of Faith-B. . . . I think that in some ages what claim to be proofs of Theism have much more effect in producing Faith-A. . . . Nearly everyone I know who has embraced Christianity in adult life has been influenced by what seems to him to be at least probable arguments for Theism. . . . Even quite uneducated people who have been Christians all their lives not infrequently appeal to some simplified form of the Argument from Design. Even acceptance of tradition implies an argument which sometimes becomes explicit in the form "I reckon all those wise men wouldn't have believed in it if it weren't true."[8]

However, as Lewis points out elsewhere, our age is different from many previous ages in that many people are half-educated: not wise enough to assess the arguments for God, not simple enough to trust "all those wise men" who have. Therefore, in our days a number of Christians are confused about their grounds for belief. When their faith is challenged, they either abandon their commitment or retreat to a sort of stubborn insistence: "Don't confuse me with arguments; I *know* it's true."

But the *appetite* for argument exists in the ordinary Christian, which accounts for a good deal of Lewis's own popularity: he gives rational backing to the inarticulate certainty of many ordinary Christians that their faith is true and to be trusted.

7. Rivals of Christianity

At some point, any defender of Christianity has to answer the question, "Why Christianity and not some other religious belief?" This question has been answered to some extent in the earlier chapters, and we have made these key points:

1. Only the Christian doctrine of the Trinity gives a real idea of a God *"beyond* personality," *more* than personal.
2. Only Christ, of all great religious teachers, has claimed to be the Son of God, and backed up this claim with miracles.
3. Only the idea of the faithful as the "Body of Christ," suffering with and in Christ for the redemption of all, can provide an adequate answer to the problem of suffering.

Lewis's main concern was to support Christianity, not to undermine any other religions. However, in defending Christianity he did make some negative points about other religions, and about such quasi-religious views as humanism. Because criticism of other religions is often identified as "intolerance," which raises the specter of persecution, before I begin discussing these issues I want to make it clear that Lewis was completely opposed to religious persecution—and, indeed, to any compulsion in religious matters. He believed that, although the ideal might be for all people to be Christians, God is certainly willing and able to save those who never hear of Christianity or who reject it through no fault of their own.

As he wrote to Bede Griffiths:

I sometimes have the feeling that the big mass-conversions of the Dark Ages, often carried out by force, were all a false dawn and the whole work has to be done over again. As for the virtuous heathen, we are told that Our Lord is the savior "of all men" though "specifically of those who believe." As there is vicarious suffering, is there not also vicarious faith?[1]

Lewis was especially likely to discuss the problem of the sincere disbeliever with Griffiths, his friend and former student who had become a Roman Catholic, for there is some evidence that Griffiths attempted to persuade Lewis to become a Catholic. Lewis replied with a defense of his own position, which very likely expressed in reverse what he felt about Griffiths:

The doctrine held by your own Church about the position of the virtuous heretic or pagan . . . [is] that many who have lived and died outside the visible Church are finally saved, because Divine Grace has guided them to concentrate solely on the true elements in their own religion. And if so, must one not admit that it was the mysterious will of God that these persons should be saved in that peculiar way?[2]

In *The Last Battle,* the final book of the *Chronicles of Narnia,* Lewis gives a striking fictional portrayal of a person saved by concentrating on the true elements in a false religion. *The Last Battle* is an apocalyptic tale of the last days of Narnia, in which an ape named Shift starts a false religion by dressing a donkey in a lion's skin to impersonate Aslan, the great lion who is in Narnia what Christ is in our world: God incarnate. The enemy of Narnia is a quasi-Persian nation called Calormen, whose official religion is the worship of the cruel bird-headed god Tash, who demands human sacrifice and other abominations. As spokesman of the false Aslan, Shift eventually preaches that Tash and Aslan are really one: a composite god he calls Tashlan. The Calormenes, who are skeptical about their own god, go along with this story in order to take over Narnia.

But one young soldier, Emeth, is shocked by the cynicism of his fellow Calormenes. He believes in Tash, though he has concentrated on Tash's awesomeness, not on his cruelty. When Shift and the Calormene leader pretend for their own purposes that Tash is in a certain building—where, in fact, a soldier is lurking to kill anyone bold enough to test the claim—Emeth insists on entering the building to come face to face with the god he loves, and he is killed.

The concluding chapters of *The Last Battle* take place in a world of life after death, where some of the principal characters encounter Emeth wandering, happy but dazed. Here is his account of what happened to him after his death:

[In] a narrow place between two rocks there came to meet me a great Lion. The speed of him was like the ostrich, and his size was an elephant's; his hair was like pure gold and the brightness of his eyes like gold that is liquid in the furnace. He was more terrible than the Flaming Mountain of Lagour, and in beauty he surpassed all that is in the world, even as the rose in bloom surpasses the dust of the desert. Then I fell at his feet and thought, Surely this is the hour of death, for the Lion (who is worthy of all honour) will know that I have served Tash all my days and not him. Nevertheless, it is better to see the Lion and die than to be Tisroc of the world and live and not to have seen him. But the Glorious One bent down his golden head and touched my forehead with his tongue and said, Son, thou art welcome. But I said, Alas, Lord, I am no son of Thine but the servant of Tash. He answered, Child, all the service thou hast done to Tash, I account as service done to me. Then by reason of my great desire for wisdom and understanding, I overcame my fear and questioned the Glorious One and said, Lord, is it then true, as the Ape said, that thou and Tash are one? The Lion growled so that the earth shook (but his wrath was not against me) and said, It is false. Not because he and I are one, but because we are opposites, I take to me the services which thou hast done to him, for I and he are of such different kinds that no service which is vile can be done to me, and none which is not vile can be done to him. Therefore if any man swear by Tash and keep his oath for the oath's sake, it is by me that he has truly sworn, though he know it not, and it is I who reward him. And if any man do a cruelty in my name, then though he says the name Aslan, it is Tash whom he serves and by Tash his deed is accepted. Dost thou understand, Child? I said, Lord, thou knowest how much I understand. But I said also (for the truth constrained me), Yet I have been seeking Tash all my days.

Beloved, said the Glorious One, unless thy desire had been for me thou wouldst not have sought so long and so truly. For all find what they truly seek.[3]

Notice that even those who serve an evil god are judged by their good intentions, while those who do evil in the name of the true God are condemned. A desire of a particular kind for a false god is, in fact, a desire for the true God. All of this is part of Lewis's answer to the problem of the millions of people who have had no fair chance to accept the Christian message.

Since some of Lewis's traditionalist admirers have been a little uneasy about the view expressed in *The Last Battle,* and have tried to weaken or reinterpret its message, it may be well to quote Lewis's more explicit thoughts on the subject:

I think that every prayer that is made even to a false God or to the very imperfectly conceived true God is accepted by the true God, and that Christ saves many who do not think they know Him. For He is (dimly) present in the *good* side of the inferior teachers whom they follow. In the parable of the sheep and goats (Matt. 25:3 and following) those who are saved do not seem to know they have served Christ. But of course our anxiety about unbelievers is most perfectly employed when it leads not to speculation but to earnest prayer for them and the attempt to be in our own lives such good advertisements for Christianity as will make it attractive.[4]

If God will save non-Christians, then why the worry about missionary work, about "preaching the Gospel to all nations"? Partly because it is always better to know the truth than to be in darkness, partly because someone who is working under the handicap of ignorance or false ideas is less effective in doing God's work. But most of all because Christians have orders from their Master to preach and baptize.

Without giving any detailed critique of other religions, Lewis indicates the general lines on which such a critique could be constructed. He saw Hinduism and Christianity as the two major religious traditions, with Buddhism a variant of Hinduism and Islam a variant of the Judeo-Christian tradition. He made several general criticisms of Hinduism, the first having to do with the basic Hindu idea that the proper destiny of the human soul is to lose its self-identity and be somehow absorbed into God. Lewis saw this as a reversion to a stage before the world was created as a reality separate from God.

> We all once existed potentially in Him and in that sense were not other than He. And even now inorganic matter has a sort of unity with Him that we lack. To what end was creation except to separate us in order that we may be reunited to Him in that unity of love which is utterly different from mere numerical identity and indeed presupposes that the lover and the beloved be distinct? Thus the whole Indian aim seems to be backward towards a sort of unity which God deliberately rejected and not outward to the true one.[5]

This, of course, assumes the Christian view that God has created the universe as something separate from himself: Lewis would have argued that this was the truth; and, indeed, it can be difficult to understand what is meant by the Hindu idea. A drop of water can be separated from, then reabsorbed into a larger body of water, but what does it mean to say that a person is "absorbed" into God? The idea seems to conceal a primitive notion of "soul-stuff" as something quasi-material.

Another criticism Lewis made of Hinduism was its separation of what Lewis called the "thick" and "clear" elements of religion.

> By Thick I mean those which have orgies and ecstasies and local attachments: Africa is full of Thick religions.
>
> By Clear I mean those which are philosophical, ethical and universalizing: Stoicism, Buddhism and the Ethical Church are Clear religions. Now if there is a true religion it must be both Thick and Clear for the true God must have made both the child and the man, both the savage and the citizen, both the head and the belly. And the only two religions that satisfy this condition are Hinduism and Christianity. But Hinduism fulfills it imperfectly. The Clear religion of the Brahman hermit in the jungle and the Thick religion of the neighboring temple go on *side by side.* The Brahman hermit doesn't bother about the temple prostitution nor the worshipper in the temple about the hermit's metaphysics. But Christianity really breaks down the middle wall of the partition. It takes a

convert from central Africa and teaches him to obey an enlightened universalist ethic: it takes a twentieth-century academic prig like me and tells me to go fasting to a Mystery, to drink the blood of the Lord. The savage convert has to be Clear: I have to be Thick. That is how one knows one has come to the real religion.[6]

In Lewis's last and perhaps greatest novel, *Till We Have Faces,* he gives a graphic illustration of his point about thick and clear religions. The protagonist, Orual, is first princess then Queen of Glome, a barbaric kingdom on the edges of Hellenic civilization in a period perhaps a few centuries before Christ. The official religion of Glome is the worship of Ungit, a fertility goddess whose worship involves temple prostitution and animal and sometimes human sacrifice. Orual's tutor is a Greek slave nicknamed the Fox, who tries to teach her ethical and philosophical doctrines that are essentially those of Stoicism.*

When the old priest of Ungit dies, Arnom, the new priest, (under the influence of the Fox) replaces the old shapeless stone image of Ungit with a new statue in the Greek style and begins to allegorize the old beliefs. In a sort of vision near the end of the book, Orual stands before the gods, and the Fox defends her to them in these words:

Oh, Minos, or Rhadamanthus, or Persephone, or by whatever name you are called, I am to blame for most of this, and I should bear the punishment. I taught her, as men teach a parrot, to say, "Lies of poets," and "Ungit's a false image." I made her think that ended the question. I never said, Too true an image of the demon within. And then the other face of Ungit (she has a thousand) . . . something live anyway. And the real gods more alive. Neither they nor Ungit mere thoughts or words. I never told her why the old Priest got something from the dark House that I never got from my trim sentences. She never asked me (I was content she shouldn't ask) why the people got something from the

---

*Stoicism, which Lewis mentions as his first example of a clear religion in the passage just quoted, was an ethical-religious view that held to the belief in one God and in the brotherhood of man, and tried to demythologize the popular religion by explaining the gods and goddesses as allegorical representations of philosophical and ethical truths.

shapeless stone which no one ever got from that painted doll of
Arnom's. Of course, I didn't know; but I never told her I didn't know.
I don't know now. Only that the way to the true gods is more like the
house of Ungit . . . oh, it's unlike too, more unlike than we yet dream,
but that's the easy knowledge, the first lesson; only a fool would stay
there, posturing and repeating it. The Priest knew at least that there
must be sacrifices. They will have sacrifice—will have man. Yes, and the
very heart, center, ground, roots of a man; dark and strong and costly
as blood. Send me away, Minos, even to Tartarus, if Tartarus can cure
glibness. I made her think that a prattle of maxims would do, all thin and
clear as water. For of course water's good; and it didn't cost much, not
where I grew up. So I fed her on words.[7]

Here a representative of clear religion is used to make the point
about thick and clear that Lewis has made in an abstract way in
the passage quoted earlier: true religion must include both thick
and clear elements; the clear religions make religion too much a
matter of intellectual assent and ignore the necessary commitment in faith, which at its highest point becomes the necessity for
sacrifice, the offering of "the very heart, center, ground, and
roots of a man" to God.

The kinds of religious belief we have discussed so far are what
we ordinarily think of as "religions." But many people in the
modern world subscribe to what may be called a religion in a
wider sense: a world view combined with an ethical position. We
will discuss three such quasi-religious belief systems: first, what
I will call the cosmic world view; second, what I will call the
psychoanalytic world view; and, finally, communism. The cosmic
world view is neatly caricatured in the following passage:

Supposing this to be a myth, is it not one of the finest myths which
human imagination has yet produced? The play is preceded by the most
austere of all preludes: the infinite void, and matter restlessly moving to
bring forth it knows not what. Then, by the millionth millionth chance
—what tragic irony—the conditions at one point of space and time
bubble up into that tiny fermentation which is the beginning of life.
. . . But life somehow wins through. With infinite suffering, against all
but insuperable obstacles, it spreads, it breeds, it complicates itself; from

the amoeba up to the plant, up to the reptile, up to the mammal . . . amidst the beasts that are far larger and stronger than he, there comes forth a little naked, shivering, cowering creature, shuffling, not yet erect, promising nothing: the product of another millionth millionth chance. Yet somehow he thrives. . . . He learns to master Nature. Science comes and dissipates the superstitions of his infancy. More and more he becomes the controller of his own fate. Passing hastily over the present (for it is mere nothing by the time-scale we are using), you follow him on into the future. See him in the last act, though not the last scene, of this great mystery. A race of demigods now rule the planet—and perhaps more than the planet—for eugenics have made certain that only demigods will be born, and psycho-analysis that none of them shall lose or smirch his divinity, and communism that all which divinity requires shall be ready to their hand. Man has ascended his throne. Henceforward he has nothing to do but practice virtue, to grow in wisdom, to be happy. And now, mark the final stroke of genius. If the myth stopped at that point, it might be a little bathetic. It would lack the highest grandeur of which human imagination is capable. The last scene reverses all. We have the Twilight of the Gods. All this time, silently, unceasingly, out of all reach of human power, Nature, the old enemy, has been steadily gnawing away. The sun will cool—all suns will cool—the whole universe will run down. Life (every form of life) will be banished, without hope of return, from every inch of infinite space. All ends in nothingness, and "universal darkness covers all."[8]

Along with the world view in question is an ethical attitude: that the survival of the human race is the highest value, and whatever serves that value is good. As Lewis wrote to Bede Griffiths:

I was talking the other day to an intelligent infidel who said he pinned his hopes for any significance in the universe on the chance that the human race by adapting itself to changed conditions and first planet jumping, then star jumping, could really last forever and subject matter wholly to mind. When I said it was overwhelmingly improbable he said, Yes but one had to believe even in the 1000th chance or life was mockery. I of course asked why, feeling like that, he did not prefer to believe in the other and traditional "chance" of a spiritual immortality. To that he replied—obviously not for effect but producing something that had long been in his mind—"Oh I never can believe that, for if *that* were true our having a physical existence is so pointless." He's a nice, honest chap, and I have no doubt at all that this is one of the things standing between him and Christianity.[9]

The point of view of this "intelligent infidel" is given to Weston, the scientist-villain in *Out of the Silent Planet*. Defending his ideals to Oyarsa, an angelic being who rules the planet Malacandra (Mars), Weston gives a speech, the logical flaws in which are brought out by the attempts of Ransom, the book's protagonist, to translate them into the language of Mars. Ransom himself has only a limited grasp of this language and thus has to translate impressive verbiage into revealingly simple equivalents:

As soon as Ransom finished, Weston continued.

"Life is greater than any system of morality: her claims are absolute. It is not by tribal taboos and copy-book maxims that she has pursued her relentless march from the amoeba to man and from man to civilization."

"He says," began Ransom, "that living creatures are stronger than the question whether an act is bent or good—no, that cannot be right—he says it is better to be alive and bent than to be dead—no—he says, he says—I cannot say what he says, Oyarsa, in your language. But he goes on to say that the only good thing is that there should be very many creatures alive. He says there were many other animals before the first men and the later ones were better than the earlier ones; but he says the animals were not born because of what is said to the young about bent and good action by their elders. And he says these animals did not feel any pity." . . .

"It is her right," said Weston, "the right, or, if you will, the might of Life herself, that I am prepared without flinching to plant the flag of man on the soil of Malacandra: to march on, step by step, superseding, where necessary, the lower forms of life that we find, claiming planet after planet, system after system, till our posterity—whatever strange form and yet unguessed mentality they have assumed—dwell in the universe wherever the universe is habitable."

"He says," translated Ransom, "that because of this it would *not* be a bent action—or else, he says, it *would* be a possible action—for him to kill you all and bring us here. He says he would feel no pity. He is saying again that perhaps they would be able to keep moving from one world to another and wherever they came they would kill everyone. I think he is now talking about worlds that go around other suns. He wants the creatures born from us to be in as many places as they can. He says he does not know what kind of creatures they will be."[10]

The Oyarsa's criticisms of Weston's view are criticisms Lewis himself made of plans for "interplanetary imperialism": first, the whole process is futile since the whole universe will eventually die; second, loyalty to one's own species is only part of morality and has no stronger base than its other parts—"pity and straight dealing and shame and the like." As Oyarsa says, loyalty to the human race *is* a virtue, "But if we ask you why it is a law you can give no other reason for it than for all the other and greater laws which it drives you to disobey."

Within modern science fiction a Weston-like point of view is still influential. Here is a quote from the editorial policy statement of *Destinies,* a magazine of science fact and science fiction that was one of the more influential publications in the field:

OK. It's time to come out front and admit it. The evidence is in plain sight; *Destinies* is not the fun-loving magazine of science fiction and speculative fact that it purports to be, but a tool of the Space Industrialization Conspiracy, a self-appointed organ of agitprop for high technology and space exploitation.

There are, broadly speaking, two reasons for this state of affairs. One of them is based on hard-headed liberal motivations. The other is in a more abstract, philosophical vein.

The philosophical reason is unsuitable for treatment at less than tome-length. We will but note in passing: to the best of our certain knowledge (though not belief) mankind is the cutting edge of the universe's evident evolution toward self awareness. If the concept of "duty" has any meaning, it is ours to propagate ourselves throughout the universe so far as we are able, evolving ourselves and our artifacts the while to higher and higher levels of awareness: to be fruitful and multiply, to populate the universe. The logical outcome of this process is the integration of all mass and energy into a single entity (and what would *you* call such an entity?). This is the meaning of life.[11]

For many of our contemporaries this *is* the meaning of life, the only meaning life has. Both within and without the science fiction community it has begun to be pointed out that this grandiose vision ignores the present suffering and despair of countless human beings: what solace is this vision of the future for the mother of a starving baby in Africa? Furthermore, if we do encounter other intelligent beings in the universe, will we exploit and ruin them as contemporary Western civilization has done with so many ancient cultures? The grand vision either embraces this possibility or is silent about it. Lewis's was one of the first voices raised against "interplanetary imperialism"; his voice remains one of the most eloquent.

The psychoanalytic world view goes to the other extreme from the cosmic: it makes individual "adjustment," individual happiness, the highest value to which it sacrifices all other values. The proponents of the cosmic world view want to conquer outer space; the proponents of the psychoanalytic world view speak metaphorically of the conquest of "inner space," our minds. Part of Lewis's critique of "the religion of happiness" was that no finite satisfaction will really satisfy our "infinite longings." When moderns speak of "personal fulfillment," they often have sexual fulfillment in mind, and Lewis points out what experience tells us about sexual passion:

> It is part of the nature of a strong erotic passion—as distinct from a transient fit of appetite—that it makes more towering promises than any other emotion. No doubt all our desires make promises, but not so impressively. To be in love involves the almost irresistible conviction that one will go on being in love until one dies, and that possession of the beloved will confer, not merely frequent ecstasies, but settled, fruitful, deep-rooted, lifelong happiness. Hence *all* seems to be at stake. If we miss this chance we shall have lived in vain. At the very thought of such a doom we sink into fathomless depths of self-pity.
>
> Unfortunately these promises are found often to be quite untrue. Every experienced adult knows this to be so as regards all erotic passions (except the one he himself is feeling at the moment). We discount the world-without-end pretensions of our friends' amours easily

enough. We know that such things sometimes last—and sometimes don't. And when they do last, this is not because they promised at the outset to do so. When two people achieve lasting happiness, this is not solely because they are great lovers but because they are also—I must put it crudely—good people; controlled, loyal, fair-minded, mutually adaptable people.

If we establish a "right to (sexual) happiness" which supersedes all the ordinary rules of behaviour, we do so not because of what our passion shows itself to be in experience but because of what it professes to be while we are in the grip of it. Hence, while the bad behaviour is real and works miseries and degradations, the happiness which was the object of the behaviour turns out again and again to be illusory. Everyone (except Mr. A. and Mrs. B.) knows that Mr. A. in a year or so may have the same reason for deserting his new wife as for deserting his old. He will feel again that all is at stake. He will see himself again as the great lover, and his pity for himself will exclude all pity for the woman.[12]

We have the advantage over Lewis of having lived through the 1970s—the "me decade"—and having seen the failure of system after system of behavior based on personal gratification. But again Lewis was prophetic about future intellectual trends and their dangers: the essay from which the last quote was taken appeared in the old *Saturday Evening Post* in 1963. (It was one of the last things Lewis wrote for publication.)

Thus, to the man or woman who would make "personal fulfillment" the meaning of life, Lewis would say, "Seek God, or at least seek justice and mercy, and you will often find happiness. But seek happiness directly and sacrifice everything else to it and not only will you lose everything else, you will certainly find happiness has escaped you."

Communism, or, more precisely, Marxism or dialectical materialism, has attracted many more followers and influenced history much more than either the cosmic or the psychoanalytic world view. As Lewis pointed out, Marxism appeals to our altruism by promising social justice and to our self-interest by promising its adherents that they are on the side of an inevitable historical process that must eventually triumph. As Lewis says:

[Marxism involves] two beliefs which cannot, so far as I can see, be reconciled in logic but which blend easily on the emotional level: the belief that the process which the Party embodies is inevitable and the belief that the forwarding of this process is the supreme duty and abrogates all ordinary moral laws. In this state of mind men can become devil-worshipers in the sense that they can now *honor* as well as obey their own vices. All men at times obey their vices: but it is when cruelty, envy and lust of power appear as the commands of a great super-personal force that they can be exercised with self-approval. The first symptom is in the language. When to "kill" becomes to "liquidate" the process has begun: the pseudo-scientific word disinfects the thing of blood and tears or pity and shame, and mercy itself can be regarded as a sort of untidiness.[13]

The history not only of Marxism but of all sorts of political extremism bears out Lewis's words. When a terrorist attack on a nursery school or a schoolbus can be called "a blow for national liberation," politics has become devil worship.

Thus Lewis's critique of all rivals of Christianity can be summarized as follows: all religions except Christianity are partial truths masquerading as the whole truth and drawing their power from their element of truth. The partial truths isolated from the whole truth become deadly and end up destroying themselves as well as everything else. Lewis made this point about the cosmic world view (in this passage he calls it the "scientific point of view"), but it applies equally to all the others:

The proof or verification of my Christian answer to the cosmic sum is this. When I accept Theology I may find difficulties, at this point or that, in harmonising it with some particular truths which are imbedded in the mythical cosmology derived from science. But I can get in, or allow for, science as a whole. Granted that Reason is prior to matter and that the light of that primal Reason illuminates finite minds, I can understand how men should come, by observation and inference, to know a lot about the universe they live in. If, on the other hand, I swallow the scientific cosmology as a whole, then not only can I not fit in Christianity, but I cannot even fit in science. If minds are wholly dependent on brains, and brains on bio-chemistry, and bio-chemistry (in the long run) on the meaningless influx of the atoms, I cannot understand how the thought of those minds should have any more significance than the sounds of the wind in the trees. And this is to me the final test. This is how I distinguish dreaming and waking. When I am awake I can, in some degree, account for and study my dream. The dragon that pursued me last night can be fitted into my waking world. I know that there are such things as dreams: I know that I had eaten an indigestible dinner: I know that a man of my reading might be expected to dream of dragons. But while in the nightmare I could not have fitted in my waking experience. The waking world is judged more real because it can thus contain the dreaming world: the dreaming world is judged less real because it cannot contain the waking one. For the same reason I am certain that in passing from the scientific point of view to the theological, I have passed from dream to waking. Christian theology can fit in science, art, morality, and the sub-Christian religions. The scientific point of view cannot fit in any of these things, not even science itself. I believe in Christianity as I believe that the Sun has risen not only because I see it but because by it I see everything else.[14]

8. Christian Living

Part of any case for Christianity must be a defense and recommendation of the Christian way of life. A sort of composite caricature of Christians as seen by their critics might go something like this: Christians are moralistic people who condemn vast areas of quite normal human behavior and feel themselves to be morally superior to others. They expect nonbelievers to conform to moral prohibitions that are based on Christian beliefs about what their God has arbitrarily commanded or prohibited. Their belief in God is based on wishful thinking and a desire to make themselves feel important despite their insignificant place in the universe. Christians ignore the work of this world and its challenges to concentrate on otherworldly concerns that have no relevance to the real problems and needs of their lives. In sum, Christians live in a dream world and are hopelessly out of touch with the real world.

In contrast, Lewis argued that it is the unbeliever who is out of touch with the real world. Christian morality is not an arbitrary set of commands laid down by a whimsical God but, so to speak, the operating instructions for the human machine, given by its creator. If we ignore those instructions, we will suffer inevitable consequences. Christians often fail to live up to their moral ideals, but they have sources of help in moral living that are not available outside of Christianity. Though, regrettably, many Christians are self-righteous, humility is an essential part of the Christian ideal. As to the accusation that a Christian's belief in God is based on wishful thinking, Lewis argued that everyone has wishes on both sides of the matter: human beings are not at all anxious to acknowledge their responsibility to a Being infinitely above them, who holds them accountable for their actions.

This chapter will examine Lewis's arguments on these points. I will use the common objections just cited as a framework, but the points I will bring out are addressed to Christians who want to deepen their understanding of Christian living as much as to outsiders who want to learn about or challenge the Christian way of life. As Lewis himself said, "A man can't always be defending the truth; there must be a time to feed on it."[1]

The place to begin is with the question of whether the moral law should be seen by Christians as the arbitrary commands of God. The answer to this problem by Lewis and by the main Christian tradition comes out most strongly in Lewis's discussion of the moral point of view in the Psalms:

When the poets call the directions or "rulings" of Jahveh "true" they are expressing the assurance that these, and not those others, are the "real" or "valid" or unassailable ones; that they are based on the very nature of things and the very nature of God.

By this assurance they put themselves, implicitly, on the right side of a controversy which arose far later among Christians. There were in the eighteenth century terrible theologians who held that "God did not command certain things because they are right, but certain things are right because God commanded them." To make the position perfectly clear, one of them even said that though God has, as it happens, commanded us to love Him and one another, He might equally well have commanded us to hate Him and one another, and hatred would then have been right. It was apparently a mere toss-up which he decided to do. Such a view in effect makes God a mere arbitrary tyrant. It would be better and less irreligious to believe in no God and to have no ethics than to have such an ethics and such a theology as this. The Jews of course never discuss this in abstract and philosophical terms. But at once, and completely, they assume the right view, knowing better than they know. They know that the Lord (not merely obedience to the Lord) is "righteous" and commands "righteousness" because He loves it. He enjoins what is good because He is good. Hence His laws have *emeth*, "truth," intrinsic validity, rock-bottom reality, being rooted in His own nature, and are therefore as solid as that Nature which He has created.[2]

Thus Lewis held that the moral law is based on two tenets: God's nature and the nature of what God has created. God could not have commanded us to hate rather than to love, since God, by nature is Love. But other commandments depend on the nature of what has been created. Our human nature is such that property is valuable to us and thus theft of our property is an injury to us. But if we were intelligent whales or dolphins, the notion of property might have no meaning for us and there would be no need to prohibit theft: we could not even understand the idea. Similarly, if we were intelligent turtles the notion of murder might have no meaning for us since if one turtle tries to attack another the victim can simply withdraw inside its shell.

But if morality is based on the structure of reality and that reality includes God, then we ignore the moral law at our peril. As Lewis says in *Mere Christianity:*

Every time you make a choice you are turning the central part of you, the part of you that chooses, into something a little different from what it was before. And taking your life as a whole, with all your innumerable choices, all your life long you are slowly turning this central thing either into a heavenly creature or into a hellish creature: either into a creature that is in harmony with God, and with other creatures, and with itself, or else into one that is in a state of war and hatred with God, and with its fellow-creatures, and with itself. To be the one kind of creature is heaven: that is, it is joy and peace and knowledge and power. To be the other means madness, horror, idiocy, rage, impotence, and eternal loneliness. Each of us at each moment is progressing to the one state or the other.[3]

Lewis argued that the basics of the moral law are understood in much the same way by every major human society. Apparent counterexamples given by some anthropologists are often from very small social groups or from social groups that have been influenced by unusual circumstances. The morality of the Mafia, for instance, is not a counterexample to the generalization that Americans recognize murder as wrong. As Lewis said:

[May] we not recognize in modern thought a very serious exaggeration of the ethical differences between different cultures? . . . I claim that we shall find far fewer differences of ethical injunction than is now popularly believed. In triumphant monotony the same indispensable platitudes will meet us in culture after culture. The idea that any of the new moralities now offered us would be simply one more addition to a variety already almost infinite, is not in accordance with the facts. We are not really justified in speaking of different moralities as we speak of different languages or different religions . . . I deny that we have any choice to make between clearly differentiated ethical systems. I deny that we have any power to make a new ethical system. I assert that wherever and whenever ethical discussion begins we find already before us an ethical code whose validity has to be assumed before we can even criticize it. For no ethical attack on any of the traditional precepts can be made except on the ground of some other traditional precept. You can attack the concept of justice because it interferes with the feeding of the masses, but you have taken the duty of feeding the masses from the world-wide code. You may exalt patriotism at the expense of mercy; but it was the old code that told you to love your country. You may vivisect your grandfather in order to deliver your grandchildren from cancer: but, take away traditional morality and why should you bother about your grandchildren?[4]

Lewis would have pointed out that this moral law, which he held was essentially the same in all ages and cultures, gives the instructions of the Maker of human nature to enable human beings to live in harmony with each other and to develop fully as human beings. Consider some practices prohibited by traditional morality but often regarded in our permissive society as acceptable because "they don't hurt anyone": extramarital sex, masturbation, homosexuality, even prostitution. A letter Lewis wrote to an inquirer about the moral basis for the condemnation of masturbation gives an important clue to Lewis's thinking on these points:

You rather take the line that a traditional moral principle must produce a proof of its validity before it is accepted: I rather, that it must be accepted until someone produces a conclusive refutation of it. But apart from that;—I agree that the stuff about "wastage of vital fluids" is rubbish. For me the real evil of masturbation would be that it takes an appetite which, in lawful use, leads the individual out of himself to complete (and correct) his own personality in that of another (and finally in children and even grandchildren) and turns it back; sends the man back into the person of himself, there to keep a harem of imaginary brides. And this harem, once admitted, works against his *ever* getting out and really uniting with a real woman. For the harem is always accessible, always subservient, calls for no sacrifices or adjustments, and can be endowed with erotic and psychological attractions which no real woman can rival. Among those shadowy brides he is always adored, always the perfect lover; no demand is made on his unselfishness, no mortification ever imposed on his vanity. In the end, they become merely the medium through which he increasingly adores himself. Do read Charles Williams' *Descent into Hell* and study the character of Mr. Wentworth. And it is not only the faculty of love which is thus sterilized, forced back on itself, but also the faculty of imagination. The true exercise of imagination, in my view, is (a) To help us to understand other people (b) To respond to, and, some of us, to produce art. But it has also a bad use: to provide for us, in shadowy form, a substitute for virtue, successes, distinctions etc. which ought to be sought *outside* in the real world—e.g. picturing all I'd do if I were rich instead of earning and saving. Masturbation involves this abuse of imagination in erotic matters (which I think bad in itself) and thereby encourages a similar abuse of it in all spheres. After all, almost the *main* work of life is to *come out* of our selves, out of the little, dark prison we are all born in. Masturbation is to be avoided as *all* things are to be avoided which retard this process. The danger is that of coming to *love* the prison.[5]

The point Lewis makes here about masturbation can be extrapolated to include such problems as homosexuality or prostitution. Homosexuality often is, and association with prostitutes almost always is, a refusal to "complete (and correct) [one's] own personality in that of another." The homosexual refuses to accept the other in the form of the opposite sex; and many, though not all homosexual encounters are depersonalized and depersonalizing. Both the homosexual and the person who pays prostitutes for sexual gratification avoid the normal consequences of sexual activity, children and family responsibilities.

The lack of commitment in such relationships is one major objection to them, and the most defensible homosexual relationships are those in which there is a mutual commitment. The seeker of transient sexual encounters, either heterosexual or homosexual, regards the other person as an object with which to secure gratification and often to get a feeling of power, which sometimes is enhanced by sadistic practices. The person who avoids commitment and treats others as objects increasingly lives in a solipsistic world where other people become unreal and the person becomes a pseudo-God in his or her own impoverished world.

It is worth studying the character of Wentworth in the Charles Williams novel Lewis cites. Wentworth is a self-important man who is frustrated when a rather silly young woman who has been an admirer of his seems to be turning to another man. Rather than competing for her affections, Wentworth allows himself to be entrapped by a mysterious being, a sort of witch or succubus who appears to him in the form of the girl who has rejected him, and who is "always accessible, always subservient." His obsession with this creature eventually causes Wentworth to abandon his friends, his work, and his integrity. He is, as Lewis said, trapped in the dark prison of self, and comes to love the prison.

About sexual affairs that involve some degree of real passion and even apparent commitment, but which avoid the full commitment of a permanent union, Lewis said:

When I was a youngster, all the progressive people were saying, "why all this prudery? Let us treat sex just as we treat all our other impulses." I was simple-minded enough to believe they meant what they said. I have since discovered that they meant exactly the opposite. They meant that sex was to be treated as no other impulse in our nature has ever been treated by civilized people. All the others, we admit, have to be bridled . . .

Our sexual impulses are thus being put in a position of preposterous privilege. The sexual motive is taken to condone all sorts of behavior which, if it had any other end in view, would be condemned as merciless, treacherous and unjust.[6]

Lewis saw that the present permissive attitude to sexual adventuring was a natural enough result of the loss of Christian belief and the removal of some of the former dangers of and obstacles to sexual promiscuity. He wrote to a Christian teacher in a secular school, who felt she was expected to discourage sexual activity in her pupils without "bringing in religion."

It certainly seems hard that you should be told to arm the young against Venus without calling on Christ. What do they want? I suppose the usual twaddle about bees and orchids . . . Indeed now that contraception has removed the most disasterous consequences for girls and medicine has largely defeated the worst horrors of syphilis, what argument against promiscuity is there left that would influence the young unless one brings in the whole supernatural and sacramental idea of man?[7]

And indeed the answer to the *"Playboy* (or *Playgirl)* philosophy" can only be a better philosophy: a view of human life that shows that there is more to life than sexual gratification.

About the accusation that belief in religion is based on "wishful thinking," Lewis had some characteristically wise and witty things to say. About the force of accusations of wishful thinking, he said:

It is the same with all thinking and all systems of thought. If you try to find out which are tainted by speculating about the wishes of the thinkers, you are merely making a fool of yourself. You must first find out on purely logical grounds which of them do, in fact, break down as arguments. Afterwards, if you like, go on and discover the psychological causes of the error.

In other words, you must show *that* a man is wrong before you start explaining *why* he is wrong. The modern method is to assume without discussion *that* he is wrong and then distract his attention from this (the only real issue) by busily explaining how he became so silly. . . . Thus I see my religion dismissed on the grounds that "the comfortable parson had every reason for assuring the nineteenth century worker that poverty would be rewarded in another world." Well, no doubt he had. On the assumption that Christianity is an error, I can see easily enough that some people would still have a motive for inculcating it. I see it so easily that I can, of course, play the game the other way round, by saying that "the modern man has every reason for trying to convince himself that there are no eternal sanctions behind the morality he is rejecting." For

[this] is a truly democratic game in the sense that all can play it all day long, and that it gives no unfair privilege to the small and offensive minority who reason. But of course it gets us not one inch nearer to deciding whether, as a matter of fact, the Christian religion is true or false. That question remains to be discussed on quite different grounds —a matter of philosophical and historical argument. However it were decided, the improper motives of some people, both for believing it and for disbelieving it, would remain just as they are.[8]

In fact, as Lewis said, the game of accusing your opponent of wishful thinking is one that everyone can play and no one can win: it leaves the state of the argument precisely where it was.

The accusation that Christians are out of touch with the real problems of life cannot be approached without deciding what the real problems of life are. If you hold the hedonistic philosophy that the only aim of life is to get as much enjoyment as possible before the inevitable extinction of ourselves and eventually of our species, then Christianity will seem unrealistic with its insistence on an afterlife and on duties that are more important than immediate pleasure. If, on the other extreme, you think that no one has a right to any ease or comfort until all injustice and exploitation has been done away with, you will find Christianity unrealistic in a different way; for it holds that there are other duties besides the duty of struggling for a perfect society. Indeed, Christianity is pessimistic about the possibility of a perfect society in this life.

These are probably the two major directions from which Christianity is attacked in our society. Exponents of the *"Playboy* philosophy" call Christians fools for denying themselves present enjoyments; the preachers of world revolution curse Christians for not abandoning everything to struggle for the eventual utopia.

Lewis would have begun by arguing that Christianity can include all that is sane and right in both the hedonistic and the utopian philosophies. Happiness is a perfectly legitimate human desire, and Christianity holds out hopes of infinite happiness. As Screwtape complains to Wormwood about God:

He's a hedonist at heart. All those fasts and vigils and stakes and crosses are only a facade. Or only like foam on the seashore. Out at sea, out in His sea, there is pleasure, and more pleasure. He makes no secret of it; at His right hand are "pleasures for evermore." Ugh! I don't think He has the least inkling of that high and austere mystery to which we rise in the Miserific Vision. He's vulgar, Wormwood. He has a bourgeois mind. He has filled His world full of pleasures. There are things for humans to do all day long without His minding in the least—sleeping, washing, eating, drinking, making love, playing, praying, working. Everything has to be *twisted* before it's any use to us. We fight under cruel disadvantages. Nothing is naturally on our side.[9]

Thus, Lewis would have said, Christianity is not opposed to natural happiness, but simply wants to put it in its proper place in relation to human nature and human destiny.

Similarly, the desire for a just society and the feeling that we should not ignore the sufferings of our fellow human beings is certainly part of Christianity. The New Testament is full of demands that we help those in need of our help: the parable of the sheep and the goats, in which people are judged on whether they have or have not fed the hungry, clothed the naked, consoled the afflicted; St. John's words that, if we claim to love God but hate our fellow humans, we are lying about our love for God. Especially striking are the words of the Epistle of St. James in James 2:14–17:

Now what use is it, my brothers, for a man to say he "has faith" if his actions do not correspond with it? Could that sort of faith save anyone's soul? If a fellow man or woman has no clothes to wear and nothing to eat, and one of you say, "Good luck to you, I hope you'll keep warm and find enough to eat," and yet give them nothing to meet their physical needs, what on earth is the good of that? Yet that is exactly what a bare faith without a corresponding life is like—useless and dead.

The utopian can hardly deny the immense amount of help that has been given to those in every kind of need by Christian churches and individual Christians. But the utopian's objection is that all of this merely gives first aid to a patient who needs radical surgery; by alleviating symptoms it may get in the way of a real cure. What is needed, says the utopian, is a revolutionary change in society. Despite the fact that most revolutions against tyrants have merely led to new forms of tyranny, the utopian continues to believe that *this* revolution will bring in the earthly paradise.

As opposed to the "nothing but pleasure" or "everything for the revolution" philosophies, Christianity offers to bring every part of our lives into the right relation to God. Love, marriage, and family, work and recreation, responsibilities to our neighbors and to the whole human race are all a part of it. Screwtape tells Wormwood that God wants our love for our fellow humans to begin with things closest to us and spread out from there. The efforts of the powers of evil are to push our concern away from those in need of our help here and now to a general and ineffective concern for humanity as a whole. As Lewis wrote to Bede Griffiths:

> But one mustn't assume burdens that God does not lay on us. It is one of the evils of the rapid diffusion of news that the sorrows of *all* the world come to us every morning. I think that each village was meant to feel pity for *its own* sick and poor whom it can help and I doubt if it is the duty of any private person to fix his mind on ills he cannot help. (This may even become an *escape* from works of charity we really can do to those we know). A great many people (not you) now seem to think that the mere state of being *worried* is itself meritorious. I don't think it is. We must, if it so happens, give our own lives for others; but even while we're doing it I think we're meant to enjoy Our Lord, and, in Him, our friends, our food, our sleep, our jokes, and the birds and the frosty sunrise. As about the distant, so about the future. It is very dark: but there's usually light enough for the next step or so. Pray for me always.[10]

The suggestion that some people feel that being worried is in *itself* meritorious is an especially acute insight into the temper of our times. One is sometimes uncharitably inclined to believe that, for many people, the amount of actual help given to those in need is in inverse proportion to the amount of verbalizing about the guilt we should all feel for the sorrowing of the world. Too many white middle-class members of our affluent society attend meetings or sign petitions and then feel justified, while those whose sorrows they bemoan are left unhelped. One suspects that the good Samaritan, having done all he could for the person whose needs had come to his attention, could go to sleep in peace; while perhaps the priest and the Levite who passed by the man in real need bemoaned the evils of a society that could not prevent robbery on the Jericho road.

In the way of practical help, Lewis donated two-thirds of his income to charity, and used his friend and lawyer Owen Barfield as an almoner to investigate and give aid to persons in need. On a more personal level, Lewis's brother tells a delightful anecdote.[11] On a country walk, Lewis encountered a tramp who showed some appreciation of poetry. Telling the man to wait, Lewis hurried home and returned with the gift of a book of collected verse and several bottles of beer. The beer without the book would have been patronizing, the book without the beer somewhat priggish: the combined gift from Lewis's own library and larder seems to strike just the right note of human comradeship.

The effort to "improve" others without their consent and often against their will was something that Lewis disliked intensely. In his relations with his students, his friends, and others with whom he came into contact, Lewis was available to give what help he could: if his help was not wanted, it would not be pushed on an unwilling recipient. In his efforts to help others understand and practice Christianity, Lewis always took the attitude that he was merely a fellow struggler, wrestling with the same problems as those he was trying to help. There is evidence that he took a similar attitude to his more advanced students: treating them as colleagues and deferring to them in such areas as music, where he felt their knowledge to be greater than his.

Charity towards others is a major component of the Christian life; obedience is another. First, obedience to the commandments of God: we may go beyond "mere" morality, but we cannot bypass it. After the basic demands of morality, the two great occasions of obedience are our daily work and our family obligations. Lewis appealed to St. Paul's teaching that everyone must work if they can, and not only work but produce work that is good:

We may have to earn our living by taking part in the production of objects which are rotten in quality and which, even if they were good in quality, would not be worth producing—the demand or "market" for them having been simply engineered by advertisement. Beside the waters of Babylon—or the assembly belt—we shall still say inwardly, "If I forget thee, O Jerusalem, may my right hand forget its cunning." (It will.)

And of course we shall keep our eyes skinned for any chance of escape. If we have any "choice of a career" (but has one man in a thousand any such thing?) we shall be after the sane jobs like greyhounds and stick there like limpets. We shall try, if we get the chance, to earn our living by doing well what would be worth doing even if we had not our living to earn. A considerable mortification of our avarice may be necessary. It is usually the insane jobs that lead to big money; they are often also the least laborious.[12]

During World War II, when such "frivolous" occupations as studying and teaching English literature came under fire, Lewis defended the pursuit of learning even in wartime by arguing that:

The war creates no absolutely new situation: it simply aggravates the permanent human situation so that we can no longer ignore it. Human life has always been lived on the edge of a precipice. . . . We have always to answer the question: "How can you be so frivolous and selfish as to think about anything but the salvation of human souls?" and we have, at the moment, to answer the additional question, "How can you be so frivolous and selfish as to think of anything but the war?" . . . There is no question of a compromise between the claims of God and the claims of culture, or politics, or anything else. God's claim is infinite and inexorable. You can refuse it: or you can begin to try to grant it. There is no middle way. Yet in spite of this it is clear that Christianity does not exclude any of the ordinary human activities. St. Paul tells people to get on with their jobs. He even assumes that Christians may go to dinner parties, and, what is more, dinner parties given by pagans. Our Lord attended a wedding and provided miraculous wine. Under the aegis of

His Church, and in the most Christian ages, learning and arts flourish. The solution to this paradox is, of course, well known to you. "Whether ye eat or drink or whatsoever ye do, do all to the glory of God."

All our merely natural activities will be accepted, if they are offered to God, even the humblest: and all of them, even the noblest, will be sinful if they are not. Christianity does not simply replace our natural life and substitute a new one: it is rather a new organization which exploits, to its own supernatural ends, these natural materials. No doubt, in a given situation, it demands the surrender of some, or of all, our merely human pursuits: it is better to be saved with one eye, than, having two, to be cast into Gehenna. But it does this, in a sense, *per accidens*—because in those special circumstances, it has ceased to be possible to practice this or that activity to the glory of God. There is no essential quarrel between the spiritual life and the human activities as such.[13]

"Whatever you do, do to the glory of God," is the key to Christian thinking about work. If a job is such that it cannot be offered to God, we must not do it. If there is anything, however humble, in our work that can be offered to God, we should make it the best offering we can. Christian workers should not only be honest and conscientious workers, they should be, to the last limit of their abilities, the best workers; as good at their jobs as they can be. The monastic slogan "to work is to pray" can be applied to all Christians.

Family obligations are another opportunity for us to obey God's will. The mutual obligations of parents and children, husbands and wives, and "kinfolk" of all degrees, are ways in which we can be called to live up to our Christian commitment. An example from Lewis's own life was his promise to Paddy Moore to care for Moore's mother after Paddy's death. Lewis's marriage late in life started off as an act of charity to enable a dying woman friend to remain in England: the fact that it turned into a marriage in the full sense of the word was an unexpected blessing.

Lewis held traditional views about marriage that are now very unpopular. He held that marriage is indissolvable and, as a consequence, that one partner in the marriage must have the final vote in cases of disagreement. This idea of the "headship" of the husband and the wife's duty of "obedience" has often been twisted into an excuse for tyranny on the part of husbands, or abandonment of responsibility on the part of wives. Rightly understood, Christian headship is always a call to service: "He who would be first among you must be the least and the servant of you all"(Matt. 20:26–27). Furthermore, the special relationship of husband and wife does not imply that women in general should take a secondary place to men in general, in religion or in daily life. When all of this has been said, however, there still remains something in the idea of the husband as responsible *for* the wife and the wife as responsible *to* the husband, which many moderns wish to reject. Whether they can replace this ideal with another that will be as satisfying to human needs is another matter.

Some people have seen in Lewis's late marriage to a divorced woman an inconsistency with his own principles. But Lewis's wife, Joy Davidman, had formerly been married to a man who had been married twice before. It might be argued that, if marriage is indissoluble, the man's first marriage was his only valid one and Joy Davidman was not validly married to him and thus was free to marry Lewis. Some admirers of Lewis, who could not reconcile their views on this matter with Lewis's action in marrying a divorced woman have even suggested that the marriage of Lewis and Joy Davidman was purely formal and was not consummated, but this contradicts so much indirect evidence in Lewis's published writing and in his private letters that the suggestion is almost incredible. The point would not need to be raised except that, in their efforts to "defend" Lewis from the "accusation" of contracting a real marriage with a woman who had been divorced, his "defenders" are indirectly supporting hostile critics who accuse Lewis of adopting a series of poses, of subtly falsifying his real attitudes.[14]

Satisfying work and satisfying family relationships are the sources of most happiness in life, but Lewis would have pointed out that work and family can bring us happiness only if they are brought into proper relationship to God. If we attempt to make human love an absolute source of happiness it will fail us. Everything in our lives must be offered to God, must die and be reborn in God.

9. The Problems of Prayer

Prayer poses one kind of problem for the unbelieving inquirer, another for the wavering believer, and yet another for the convinced and devout believer. For the skeptical inquirer, the question is one of evidence: if God existed, prayers to him would be answered; and if prayers are not answered, surely this counts against the existence of God. For doubtful believers, prayer presents a different but related problem. They have been taught that God answers prayer; however, they complain with various degrees of wistfulness or indignation that they have tried prayer and "it didn't work." The convinced believers have yet a different problem: they believe in God and want to approach him by prayer, but they are often uncertain as to how to go about it.

Lewis had something to say about all three of these problems, and what he had to say is part of his total case for Christianity. Let us consider first his answer to the unbeliever's problem. Can answers or lack of answers to prayer be used as evidence for or against the existence of God? Some skeptics have proposed putting "the power of prayer" to some sort of empirical test, and think that the Christian's reluctance to try such a test indicates a lack of real belief in God. Somewhat inconsistently, the skeptic often argues that if Christians do believe in prayer, it is an indication of a weakness in their characters: a lack of self-reliance, a willingness to turn over their problems to God rather than to face them head on. About these criticisms, Lewis said:

[Things] are proved not simply by experience but by those artificially contrived experiences which we call experiments. Could this be done about prayer?

I have seen it suggested that a team of people—the more the better —should agree to pray as hard as they knew how, over a period of six weeks, for all the patients in the Hospital A and none of those in Hospital B. Then you would tot up the results and see if A had more cures and fewer deaths. And I suppose you would repeat the experiment at various times and places so as to eliminate the influence of irrelevant factors.

The trouble is that I do not see how any real prayer could go on under such conditions. "Words without thoughts never to heaven go," says the King in *Hamlet*. Simply to say prayers is not to pray: otherwise a team of properly trained parrots would serve as well as men for our experiment. You cannot pray for the recovery of the sick unless the end you have in view is their recovery. But you can have no motive for desiring the recovery of all the patients in one hospital and none of those in another. You are not doing it in order that suffering should be relieved; you are doing it to find out what happens. The real purpose and the nominal purpose of your prayers are at variance. In other words, whatever your tongue and teeth and knees may do, you are not praying. The experiment demands an impossibility.[1]

What about the argument that we can see the cause of many things that happen after we have prayed for them, and therefore know that "they would have happened anyway"? Lewis points out in *The Screwtape Letters* that if God exists and is all-knowing and all powerful, then the "natural causes" that lead to the thing we prayed for are within God's control, and our prayers may well be one of the factors which God has taken into account in making that outcome rather than another occur: to God it is part of "the total problem of adapting the whole spiritual universe to the whole corporeal universe."[2]

As to the argument that the habit of petitionary prayer tends to take away our self-reliance, an answer can be seen in the parent-child analogy. A good parent does not do for a child what that child can do for itself, but is ready to step in when the child really needs help. God, says Lewis, operates in the same way: "He seems to do nothing of Himself which He can possibly delegate to His creatures. He commands us to do slowly and blunderingly what He could do perfectly in the twinkling of an eye. He allows us to neglect what He would have us do, or to fail. Perhaps we do not fully realize the problem . . . of enabling finite free wills to co-exist with Omnipotence. It seems to involve at every moment a sort of divine abdication."[3]

In Lewis's Narnian books, Aslan sometimes solves problems for the children from our world who are the protagonists of the books. But Aslan never does for the children what they can do for themselves: he steps in only when the danger they face is something that their own powers cannot overcome. In Lewis's view, this is the way the real God acts in the real world. When we realize this, there is no danger of the habit of prayer undermining a proper self-reliance.

But the whole business of asking God for things, which looms so large in the critics' objections, is only a small part of prayer for the practicing Christian. As Lewis says:

Prayer is either a sheer illusion or a personal contact between embryonic, incomplete, persons (ourselves) and the utterly concrete Person. Prayer in the sense of petition, asking for things, is a small part of it; confession and penitence are its threshold, adoration its sanctuary, the presence and vision and enjoyment of God its bread and wine. In it God shows Himself to us. That He answers prayers is a corollary—not necessarily the most important one—from that revelation. What He does is learned from what He is.[4]

When doubters who have been exposed to religion say that prayer "doesn't work," they usually seem to be thinking of petitionary prayer and, if questioned, usually reveal that they expect one of two kinds of results: they either expect certain *feelings* as a result of prayer, or they expect to have certain specific requests (e.g., a job, money, success in love) granted in a certain specific way: not just any job but *this* job, not just money for their needs but a specific sum, not just love, but the love of *this* person.

About feelings in relation to prayer, Lewis was very specific. The purpose of prayer is not to induce certain feelings in us, nor should we attempt to pray by inducing feelings in ourselves. Screwtape writes to Wormwood, advising him on how to keep his "patient" from praying effectively:

The simplest [way] is to turn their gaze away from [God] towards themselves. Keep them watching their own minds and trying to produce *feelings* there by the action of their own wills. When they meant to ask Him for charity, let them, instead, start trying to manufacture charitable feelings for themselves and not notice that this is what they are doing. When they meant to pray for courage, let them really be trying to feel brave. When they say they are praying for forgiveness, let them be trying to feel forgiven. Teach them to estimate the value of each prayer by their success in producing the desired feeling, and never let them suspect how much success or failure of that kind depends on whether they are well or ill, fresh or tired, at the moment.[5]

Of course, God will sometimes give us feelings of peace or joy in prayer, but Lewis warned against expecting these or counting on them. He wrote to an adult convert about to be received into the Anglican Church:

Accept these sensations with thankfulness as birthday cards from God, but remember that they are only greetings, not the real gift. I mean that it is not the sensations that are the real thing. The real thing is the gift of the Holy Spirit which can't usually be—perhaps not ever—experienced as a sensation or emotion.[6]

If Christianity does not promise or teach that certain feelings will accompany prayer or be caused by prayer, then the absence of such feelings can hardly be used as an argument that prayer "doesn't work." But surely Christianity does teach that God is a loving Father who will answer our requests. If he does not, is *that* evidence against Christianity? Again, it is good to remember that prayer is a *personal* interaction that can best be understood on the model that Christ so often used: a child asking a parent for something. A child is continually asking its parents for things, and good parents refuse more requests than they grant. Since human parents are imperfect, a refusal *may* indicate unwillingness or inability to grant a reasonable request. But even a perfect parent would refuse many requests. Sometimes it is better for children to do or get things for themselves, other things children ask for might be dangerous or destructive. A "no" to such requests is an indication of love and concern for the child's growth or the child's happiness.

But Lewis acknowledged that there is a problem in the New Testament about petitionary prayer. The promises seem explicit and unqualified. "Whatever you ask for in my name you will receive." True enough, the corrective is generally nearby: just as a human parent would not give a stone to a child who asked for bread, or a snake to a child who asked for a fish, so God will often not give us the stone we ask for thinking it to be bread—he gives us real bread instead. How many of us who have prayed fervently for something have been very glad in retrospect that we did not get it!

Still, a problem remains: not the problem of why God sometimes refuses us, but the problem of why the promises seem too unqualified:

[Some] intelligent but simple enquirers . . . come to us (this often happens) saying that they have been told that those who pray in faith to the Christian God will get what they ask: that they have tried it and not got what they asked: and what, please, is our explanation? Dare we say that when God promises "You shall have what you ask" He secretly means, "You shall have it if you ask for something I wish to give you"? What should we think of an earthly father who promised to give his son whatever he chose for his birthday and, when the boy asked for a bicycle gave him an arithmetic book, then first disclosing the silent reservation with which the promise was made?

Of course the arithmetic book may be better for the son than the bicycle, and a robust faith may manage to believe so. That is not where the difficulty, the sense of cruel mockery, lies. The boy is tempted, not to complain that the bicycle was denied, but that the promise of "anything he chose" was made. So with us. . . . I have no answer to my problem, though I have taken it to about every Christian I know, learned or simple, lay or clerical, within my own Communion or without.[7]

Perhaps this is partly a problem created by applying in too general a fashion statements made by Christ to those in very special circumstances. The promises that God will give *whatever* is asked of him seem to be addressed to the Apostles, and to have reference to their special mission. In Mark 11:24, Jesus said, "I tell you, then, when you ask for anything in prayer, you have only to believe it is yours and it will be granted to you." But this was said to Peter, and perhaps to the other apostles, immediately after Christ's triumphal entry into Jerusalem, and surely had reference to the carrying out of the mission Christ would entrust to the apostles. The somewhat similar language in John 17 seems also to be in the context of the mission of the Apostles. On the other hand, in the Sermon on the Mount and on other occasions when Christ is addressing "the multitude," he promises that prayers will be answered, but does not imply that each specific request will be granted. For example, in Matt. 7:8, "Everyone who asks will receive," but this is immediately followed by, "If anyone of yourselves is asked by his son for bread, will he give him a stone?" This implies that when we ask for something good, God will give us something good, but perhaps not the good we thought we needed. Matt. 7:11 points the moral, "Is not your Father in Heaven much more ready to give *wholesome* gifts to those who ask them?" (my emphasis).

Later in Matthew there is the saying, "If two of you agree over any request that you make on earth, it will be granted them by my Father." But this immediately follows, "All that you bind on earth shall be bound in heaven, and all that you loose on earth will be loosed in heaven," which mainstream Christianity has always taken to be a special commission to the Apostles.

At any rate, Lewis came to see something along those lines as at least a partial answer to this problem he set. In *Letters to Malcolm,* he writes:

It seems to me that we must conclude that such promises about prayer with faith refer to a kind or degree of faith which most believers never experience. A far inferior degree is, I hope, acceptable to God . . . absence of such faith as ensures the granting of prayer is not even necessarily a sin, for Our Lord had no such assurance when He prayed in Gethsemane.

How or why does such faith occur . . . ? My own idea is that it occurs only when the one who prays does so as God's fellow-worker, demanding what is needed for the joint work. It is the prophet's, the apostle's, the missionary's, the healer's prayer that is made with this confidence and finds the confidence justified by the event . . . it would be presumption for us . . . to imagine that we shall have any assurance which is not an illusion. . . . Our struggle is, isn't it?—to achieve and retain faith on a lower level. To believe that whether He can grant them or not, God will listen to our prayers, will take them into account.[8]

The person who prays with the kind of faith Lewis describes here may not always find prayer easy: it is something that needs effort. In the first place, the Christian will have to spend some time thinking about, meditating on, his or her belief. This may take various forms; a part of the day set aside for reading and thinking about the Scriptures and other Christian writings is possible for many, but people who are harried by family or business or other concerns may only have time to lift their minds to God in the midst of their work.

For some people, the approach to God may be through using their imagination to picture the important events in the history of salvation. Lewis made the point that, for strongly imaginative storytellers like himself, there are dangers in this method, called by some writers, the *compositio loci:*

> If I started with a *compositio loci* I should never reach the meditation. The picture would go on elaborating itself indefinitely and becoming every moment of less spiritual relevance.
>
> Yet mental images play an important part in my prayers. I doubt if any act of will or thought or emotion occurs in me without them. But they seem to help me most when they are most fugitive and fragmentary— rising and bursting like bubbles in champagne or wheeling like rooks in a windy sky: contradicting one another (in logic) as the crowded metaphors of a swift poet may do. Fix on any one, and it goes dead. You must do as Blake would do with a joy; kiss it as it flies. And then, in their total effect, they do mediate to me something very important.[9]

Meditation or thinking about God and God's work in history and in our lives will of course, lead to thanksgiving, to sorrow for our sins, and to adoration of God. That in turn will lead to prayer for others and for ourselves. Some Christians hesitate to pray for themselves and for their own needs, but as Lewis pointed out,

Christ has commanded us to do so. Besides that, reluctance to pray for ourselves may be due to less creditable motives:

> I too had noticed that our prayers for others flow more easily than those we offer on our own behalf. And it would be nice to accept your view that this just shows we are made to live by charity. I'm afraid, however, I detect too much less attractive reasons for the ease of my own intercessory prayers. One is that I am often, I believe, praying for others when I should be doing things for them. It's so much easier to pray for a bore than to go and see him. And the other is like unto it. Suppose I pray that you may be given grace to withstand your besetting sin (short list of candidates for this post will be forwarded on demand). Well, all the work has to be done by God and you. If I pray against my own besetting sin there will be work for me. One sometimes fights shy of admitting an act to be a sin for this very reason.[10]

For Lewis the beauty of nature was a reminder of God's goodness and beauty. Lewis tried to make every particular good thing a "channel of adoration," but he was especially sensitive to the good things of the natural world.

Our contacts with our fellow human beings can also be an occasion of prayer. Sometimes their goodness to us, or simply their own goodness, can be an occasion of thanks and praise; or it may be their needs that we may need to recommend to God's mercy, or some offense against ourselves that we need to try to forgive. There is a good deal of indirect evidence that Lewis kept in his prayers a good many people he met or had contact with by letter, and that he prayed most fervently for those who had in some way injured him, like the cruel schoolteacher who made a part of his childhood so unhappy.

The critic of Christianity often suspects that praying for the person in need may be an excuse for not giving them any practical help, and forgiving the evildoer may be an excuse for not doing something about their evildoing. No doubt it often is, so far are many Christians from living up to our ideals. But of course that requires an elaborate self-deception of a kind ably dissected by Lewis in *The Screwtape Letters,* where Screwtape boasts that, "I have had patients of my own so well in hand that they could be turned at a moment's notice from impassioned prayer for a wife's or son's 'soul' to beating or insulting the real wife or son without a qualm."[11]

However, if our sensibilities have not been dulled by self-deception, the normal effect of praying for another person is to make us realize that we ourselves may be the means that God has chosen to alleviate that person's problems. Even where the main problem—say, an inoperable cancer—is beyond our power to help, there may be something we can do in the way of sympathy or support. This applies especially to those who are close to us in terms of kinship or friendship, or to those with whom circumstances bring us into contact.

The highest form of prayer is the prayer of adoration, where we praise God and thank him, not for any particular gift, but for himself. Some critics have raised problems about such prayer: why should God ask us for such praise or want us to offer it? Lewis would have begun by pointing out that prayer is an acknowledgment of our own status as creatures who have received everything we have from God, and of God's worthiness to be thanked and praised. As Lewis wrote in *Reflections on the Psalms:*

[All] enjoyment spontaneously overflows into praise unless (sometimes even if) shyness or the fear of boring others is deliberately brought in to check it. The world rings with praise—lovers praising their mistresses, readers their favourite poet, walkers praising the countryside, players praising their favourite game—praise of weather, wines, dishes, actors, motors, horses, colleges, countries, historical personages, children, flowers, mountains, rare stamps, rare beetles, even sometimes politicians or scholars. . . .

I think we delight to praise what we enjoy because the praise not merely expresses but completes the enjoyment; it is its appointed consummation. It is not out of compliment that lovers keep on telling one another how beautiful they are; the delight is incomplete till it is expressed. . . . If it were possible for a created soul fully (I mean, up to the full measure conceivable in a finite being) to "appreciate," that is to love and delight in, the worthiest object of all, and simultaneously at every moment to give this delight perfect expression, then that soul would be in supreme beatitude. It is along these lines that I find it easiest to understand the Christian doctrine that "Heaven" is a state in which angels now, and men hereafter, are perpetually employed in praising God. This does not mean, as it can so dismally suggest, that it is like "being in Church." For our "services" both in their conduct and in our power to participate, are merely attempts at worship, never fully successful, often 99.9 per cent failures, sometimes total failures. We are not riders but pupils in the riding school; for most of us the falls and bruises, the aching muscles and the severity of the exercise, far outweigh those few moments in which we were, to our own astonishment, actually galloping without terror and without disaster. To see what the doctrine really means, we must suppose ourselves to be in perfect love with God —drunk with, drowned in, dissolved by, that delight which, far from remaining pent up within ourselves as incommunicable, hence hardly tolerable, bliss, flows out from us incessantly again in effortless and perfect expression, our joy no more separable from the praise in which it liberates and utters itself than the brightness it sheds. The Scotch catechism says that man's chief end is "to glorify God and enjoy Him forever." But we shall then know that these are the same thing. Fully to enjoy is to glorify. In commanding us to glorify Him, God is inviting us to enjoy Him.[12]

It will be noticed that many of the quotations from Lewis in this chapter are from *Letters to Malcolm,* one of Lewis's last and perhaps one of his best nonfiction books. Lewis was a very private man who did not find it easy to discuss his own devotional life, and was only moved to do so by the desire to help others. When, toward the end of his life, Lewis decided to write a book on prayer, it was natural for him to write the book as a series of letters to a friend in which he discusses problems about prayer not as an authority but as a fellow-seeker. His attitude towards his own thinking about prayer and practice of prayer is well captured in *Reflections on the Psalms:*

If an excuse is needed (and perhaps it is) for writing such a book, my excuse would be something like this. It often happens that two schoolboys can solve difficulties in their work for one another better than the master can. When you took the problem to a master, as we all remember, he was very likely to explain what you understood already, to add a great deal of information which you didn't want, and say nothing at all about the thing that was puzzling you. I have watched this from both sides of the net; for when, as a teacher myself, I have tried to answer questions brought to me by pupils, I have sometimes, after a minute, seen that expression settle down on their faces which assured me that they were suffering exactly the same frustration which I had suffered from my own teachers. The fellow-pupil can help more than the master because he knows less. The difficulty we want him to explain is one he has recently met. The expert met it so long ago that he has forgotten. He sees the whole subject, by now, in such a different light that he cannot conceive what is really troubling the pupil; he sees a dozen other difficulties which ought to be troubling him but aren't.

In this book, then, I write as one amateur to another, talking about difficulties I have met, or lights I have gained . . . with the hope that this might at any rate interest, and sometimes even help, other inexpert readers. I am "comparing notes," not presuming to instruct.[13]

Prayer is sometimes defined as "lifting the heart and mind to God." The great value of Lewis's writing on prayer is that though he did not neglect the heart, he satisfied the mind. Unanswered questions about prayer can get in the way of our prayer; Lewis tried to answer them. We pray better if we understand what we are doing; Lewis helped us understand. Those who do not pray can, with Lewis's help, at least see the point of prayer. Those of us who do pray will pray better for having read Lewis.

10. Death and Beyond

That non-Christians have rejected a belief in life after death is not surprising: Lewis argued in several places that a mere belief in "survival" of some kind, separated from a belief in God, is not fundamentally a religious belief and has very little chance of remaining as a part of a belief system divorced from a total religious world view. But one characteristic of much "liberal" or "modernist" Christianity has been the rejection of life after death as part of Christian belief. This is associated in part with a "minimizing" trend in modernism, a rejection of everything that seems incompatible with "science" or "modern consciousness." However, certain specific arguments have been given by the modernists against the idea of survival as part of Christian belief. These might be summarized under the headings of ethical, historical, and philosophical arguments.

The ethical arguments take the general line that a desire for personal immortality is somehow selfish: that we should serve God because God is good and worthy of our service, not because we hope for some reward. Lewis would have said that this argument gains its strength from a misunderstood truth: God must not be seen merely as a means to survival after death, to an immortality that has a value apart from God. On this subject, Lewis alludes to Tyndale, the sixteenth-century Protestant theologian and Bible translator:

> Tyndale as regards the natural condition of humanity [holds that] by nature we can "do no good works without respect of some profit either in this world or the world to come." . . . That the profit should be located

in another world means, as Tyndale clearly sees, no difference. Theological hedonism is still hedonism. Whether the man is seeking heaven or a hundred pounds he can still "but seek himself." Of freedom in the true sense—of spontaneity or disinterestedness—Nature knows nothing. And yet by a terrible paradox such disinterestedness is precisely what the moral law demands. . . .[1]

Tyndale's solution to the "terrible paradox" was to say that God's grace completely changes human nature; the modernist solution is to eliminate the paradox by eliminating the promise of heavenly reward. Lewis regarded both attempts as misguided, but acknowledged that they were attempted solutions to a real problem. To serve God "for pay," merely for the sake of some promised reward, seems contrary to morality and indeed contrary to what Christianity teaches about morality. In a controversy with the philosopher H. H. Price, who attempted to define religion as "belief in God and immortality," Lewis denied that a belief in immortality was essential to religion:

I do not define the essence of religion as a belief in God and immortality. Judaism in its earliest stages had no belief in immortality and for a long time no belief that was religiously relevant. . . . I cannot sufficiently admire the divine tact of thus training the chosen race for centuries without even hinting the shining secret of eternal life. He behaves like the rich lover in a romance who woos the maiden on his own merits disguised as a poor man and only when he has won her reveals that he has a throne and palace to offer. For I cannot help thinking that any religion which begins with a thirst for immortality is damned, as a religion, from the outset. Until a certain spiritual level has been reached, the promise of immortality will always operate as a bribe which vitiates the whole religion and infinitely inflames those very self-regards which religion must cut down and uproot. For the essence of religion in my view is the thirst for an end higher than natural ends: the finite self's desire for and acquiescence in, and self-rejection in favor of, an object wholly good and wholly good for it. That the self-rejection will also turn out to be a self-finding, that bread cast upon the waters will be found after many days, that to die is to live—these are sacred paradoxes which the human race must not be told too soon.[2]

Elsewhere, Lewis expresses thankfulness that his own spiritual history followed the same pattern, that he himself believed in God for some time without believing in immortality.

Thus, insofar as the modernist view arises from the rejection of immortality as a bribe, of a nonreligious thirst for mere survival, Lewis is in sympathy with it. But merely rejecting immortality is too simple a solution. First, it flies in the face of the whole New Testament and of most of Christian tradition. Second, it is an elitist view in precisely the sense in which elitist views are objectionable: because something is satisfactory to a favored minority, it is held to be satisfactory for all. Even a very inadequate Christian may feel "God has been so good to me that even if I were to be annihilated tonight I would be infinitely grateful for what existence I have had." But this leaves out a very great part of the human race that has never had the opportunities for truth and life and service that make the Christian feel that way. The slaves, the serfs, the beggars, the oppressed of all times have seemed to have good reason to "curse God and die." It is no use telling them that everything is really all right: unless they have some greater life after death, things are *not* all right for them.

Finally, the denial of immortality takes away from the goodness of God. The traditional Christian God who wants his creatures to live forever with him has a kind of goodness that the modernist version of God lacks. The modernist God seems to be saying, "I see that everything is good, everything is part of a great plan. Those who don't see it that way *could* have seen it that way and been happy." But even apart from the implausibility of the claim that all of the innocent sufferers in history *could* have been happy if they had chosen faith or acceptance, this modernist God is not the Christian God who loves each individual uniquely and infinitely, but the stoic God who says in effect, "Take the correct attitude and be happy or the wrong one and be unhappy: it is up to you, not to me." The multitudes who die in misery without any opportunity to know of reconciliation in Christ surely make this modernist God a monster; the atheist who rejects such a God is infinitely more pleasing to the real God than the theologian who piously accepts such ideas.

We are left, then, with the original terms of the problem: morality—and, indeed, Christian morality—requires that we do
good simply because it is good. But if God promises us any
reward (and "peace" in this life is just as much a reward as
heaven), how can our service be solely for the sake of good?

The solution lies in a distinction between different kinds of
rewards. What might be called "external" rewards have no essential relation to what they are rewards for: they are merely "added
on." Giving a child a bicycle for getting good grades or promising
someone a sum of money to marry someone else would be examples. However, some rewards are "internal" rewards, they have
an essential connection with the activities that earn them. For
example, a scholarship for further study given on the basis of
good grades, or a life of married happiness as a "reward" for
marrying the right person.

Of course, internal rewards can appear from a certain point of
view to be external; a scholarship, after all, has a monetary value
and a happy marriage is a period of happiness. Sometimes in fact,
an internal reward may at first be seen as external. This can be
brought out by a small parable. George, who hated cats, had a
rich aunt who loved them. To impress her he pretended to be a
cat lover, learned a great deal about cats, and acquired several
cats of his own. Eventually, the aunt died and left her money to
George in trust, to build and manage a home for stray cats. The
story could have a sad or a happy ending. The sad ending is a
frustrated George, condemned to keep associating with animals
he detests in order to get any benefit at all from his aunt's will.
The happy ending is a George who, by pretending to love cats,
has actually acquired a fondness for them and is really pleased
with his aunt's will.

Many Christians are in a position similar to George's with
regard to heaven. We start by seeking heaven as an external
reward, and there may be some pretence about how much we
really want it. But as we live in the way that we hope will gain us
this reward, we gradually begin to become the sort of people who
can appreciate heaven. For, of course, real hypocrisy about an
internal reward is self-defeating. A student who hates to study is

not rewarded by a scholarship; it only means more of an uncongenial activity. Unless you love a person, spending your life with her or him is not a reward but a punishment. And since Heaven is essentially being with God, unless we love God heaven is no reward. Within the "logic of personal relations," the distinction between external and internal rewards makes perfect sense; we can see the insanity of an "unselfishness" that would reject being with the loved one because the happiness it brings would be a "bribe." As Lewis says in *The Problem of Pain:*

[We] are afraid that heaven is a bribe, and that if we make it our goal we shall no longer be disinterested. It is not so. Heaven offers nothing that a mercenary soul can desire. It is safe to tell the pure in heart that they shall see God, for only the pure in heart want to. There are rewards that do not sully motives. A man's love for a woman is not mercenary because he wants to marry her, nor his love for poetry mercenary because he wants to read it, nor his love of exercise less disinterested because he wants to run and leap and walk. Love, by definition, seeks to enjoy its object.[3]

This seems to dispose of the ethical argument and also of the historical argument, which argues that belief in an afterlife was a "late development" in Judaism that was due to "Hellenic influences" rather than to the "Hebrew spirit." Unless it can be proven that anything in Christianity that is due to Hellenic rather than Hebrew ways of thought is thereby discredited, these alleged facts have no weight. To the contrary, Lewis saw a process of gradual development in the Old Testament:

When God began to reveal Himself to men, to show them that He and nothing else is their goal and the satisfaction of their needs, and that He has a claim upon them simply by being what He is, quite apart from anything He can bestow or deny, it may have been absolutely necessary that this revelation should not begin with any hint of future Beatitude or Perdition. These are not the right points to begin at. An effective belief in them, coming too soon, may even render almost impossible the development of (so to call it) the appetite for God; personal hopes and fears, too obviously exciting, have got in first. Later, when, after centuries of spiritual training, men have learned to desire and adore God, to pant after Him "as pants the hart," it is another matter. For then those who love God will desire not only to enjoy Him but "to enjoy Him forever," and will fear to lose Him. And it is by that door that a truly religious hope of Heaven and fear of Hell can enter; as corollaries to a faith already centred upon God, not as things of any independent or intrinsic weight. It is even arguable that the moment "Heaven" ceases to mean union with God and "Hell" to mean separation from Him, the belief in either is a mischievous superstition; for then we have, on the one hand, a merely "compensatory" belief (a "sequel" to life's sad story, in which everything will "come all right") and, on the other, a nightmare which drives men into asylums or makes them persecutors.

Fortunately, by God's good providence, a strong and steady belief of that self-seeking and sub-religious kind is extremely difficult to maintain, and is perhaps possible only to those who are slightly neurotic. Most of us find that our belief in the future life is strong only when God is in the centre of our thoughts; that if we try to use the hope of "Heaven" as a compensation (even for the most innocent and natural misery, that of bereavement) it crumbles away. It can, on those terms, be maintained only by arduous efforts of controlled imagination; and we know in our hearts that the imagination is our own.

All this is only one man's opinion. And it may be unduly influenced by my own experience. For I (I have said it in another book, but the repetition is unavoidable) was allowed for a whole year to believe in God and try—in some stumbling fashion—to obey Him before any belief in the future life was given me. And that year always seems to me to have been of very great value. It is therefore perhaps natural that I should suspect a similar value in the centuries during which the Jews were in the same position. Other views no doubt can be taken.[4]

The philosophical arguments against immortality begin by alleging certain difficulties in the idea of a disembodied spirit. If, as some philosophers allege, this is incoherent or self-contradictory, then we cannot make sense of the idea of surviving as a disembodied soul and can base our hope of immortality only on the idea of resurrection. But if resurrection consists only in the recreation of our bodies and our memories of some future time and place, a problem arises: in what sense would *we*, rather than just a duplicate of ourselves, live at this future time?

By eliminating any continuing existence for us between death and resurrection, the "resurrection only" view does seem to create such a difficulty. In the traditional view on which our spirit continues to exist in a disembodied state between death and resurrection, there is no gap in existence and the "new" body is animated by the "same old" spirit, thus eliminating the question, "Is this me or a duplicate of me?" Lewis, as might be expected, defended the traditional view: he saw no difficulties in the idea of a disembodied spirit which could not be overcome.

A brief recapitulation of the traditional doctrine may prevent some misunderstandings here. The traditional view, derived from philosophical reflection on scriptural revelation, holds that there are two kinds of real existence: matter and spirit. Rocks and rivers are purely material; they occupy space and are subject to such physical laws as gravitational attraction. God and angels are purely spiritual; they have no location in space and are not subject to the laws that govern the behavior of matter. Human beings are both material and spiritual; our bodies are matter, but our minds are spirit. Thus, we have direct acquaintance with both realms of reality. Activities such as running require a body; activities such as thinking require a spirit. Human beings can both run and think. Angels can think but not run, rivers can run but not think. Human beings are thus intended to be the meeting place of matter and spirit, and a human without a body is not fully human.

This is opposed to the view, held by the philosopher Plato and his followers, that humans are essentially spirits and our bodies are prisons from which death releases us. The importance of resurrection is that it restores the unity of body and spirit that was lost at death.

In *Letters to Malcolm,* Lewis speculated about how we might best understand the idea of resurrection:

About the resurrection of the body. I agree with you that the old picture of the soul reassuming the corpse—perhaps blown to bits or long since usefully dissipated through nature—is absurd. Nor is it what St. Paul's words imply. And I admit that if you ask what I substitute for this, I have only speculations to offer. . . .

What the soul cries out for is the resurrection of the senses. Even in this life matter would be nothing to us if it were not the source of sensations.

Now we already have some feeble and intermittent power of raising dead sensations from the graves. I mean, of course, memory.

You see the way my thought is moving. But don't run away with the idea that when I speak of the resurrection of the body I mean merely that the blessed dead will have excellent memories of their sensuous experiences on earth. I mean it the other way round: that memory as we now know it is a dim foretaste, a mirage even, of a power which the soul, or rather Christ in the soul (he "went to prepare a place for us") will exercise hereafter. It need no longer be intermittent. Above all, it need no longer be private to the soul in which it occurs. I can now communicate to you the vanished fields of my boyhood—they are building-estates today—only imperfectly by words. Perhaps the day is coming when I can take you for a walk through them . . . the hills and valleys of Heaven will be to those you now experience not as a copy is to an original, nor as a substitute to the genuine article, but as the flower to the root, or the diamond to the coal.

I don't say the resurrection of this body will happen at once. It may well be that this part of us sleeps in death and the intellectual soul is sent to Lenten lands where she fasts in naked spirituality—a ghostlike and imperfectly human condition. I don't imply that an angel is a ghost. But naked spirituality is in accordance with his nature: not, I think, with ours. (A two-legged horse is maimed but not a two-legged man.) Yet from that fact my hope is that we shall return and re-assume the wealth we laid down.

Then the new earth and sky, the same yet not the same as these, will rise in us as we have risen in Christ. And once again, after who knows what aeons of the silence and the dark, the birds will sing out and the waters flow, and lights and shadows move across the hills and the faces of our friends laugh upon us with amazed recognition.

Guesses, of course, only guesses. If they are not true, something better will be. For we know that we shall be made like Him, for we shall see Him as He is.[5]

Lewis did not deal with some of the specific philosophical objections to the idea of disembodied survival: indeed, some of the subtler ones have been developed since his death. But the course of philosophical controversy seems to show that no objection is fatal to the idea of disembodied survival, and the most convincing of them often depend on a view of philosophy or a view of language that is in itself open to objection. On the popular level, the objection to disembodied survival is more a matter of imagination—of ability to imagine what a disembodied existence would be *like*, than it is a matter of any specific objection.

Indeed, probably the major barrier to belief in life after death is more a matter of imagination than of argument. The symbols and images that we inherit from the Old and New Testaments are designed for a different sort of imagination than ours, an oriental rather than an occidental imagination. In his discussion of medieval literature, Lewis says of Jean de Meun's picture of heaven in *The Romance of the Rose:* "No one who remembers the falsity of most poetical attempts to describe Heaven—the dull catalogues of jewelry and mass-singing—will underrate this green park, with its unearthly peace, its endless sunshine and fresh grass and grazing flocks."[6]

Except for the "grazing flocks," this is very much the picture of heaven given in most of Lewis's imaginative works. Here is a description of "Aslan's Country" from *The Silver Chair,* when Jill Pole and Eustace Scrubb first enter it from our world:

[There] was a quite different sound all about them. It came from those bright things overhead, which now turned out to be birds. They were making a riotous noise, but it was much more like music—rather advanced music which you don't quite take in at the first hearing—than birds' songs ever are in our world. Yet, in spite of the singing, there was a sort of background of immense silence. That silence, combined with the freshness of the air, made Jill think they must be on the top of a very high mountain.

Scrubb still had her by the hand and they were walking forward, staring about them on every side. Jill saw that huge trees, rather like cedars but bigger, grew in every direction. But as they did not grow close together, and as there was no undergrowth, this did not prevent one from seeing a long way into the forest to left and right. And as far as Jill's eye could reach, it was all the same—level turf, darting birds with yellow, or dragonfly blue, or rainbow plumage, blue shadows, and emptiness. There was not a breath of wind in that cool, bright air.[7]

In an essay entitled "The Weight of Glory," Lewis summarizes the promises of Scripture with regard to the afterlife:

> The promise of Scripture may very roughly be reduced to five heads. It is promised, firstly, that we shall be with Christ; secondly, that we shall be like Him; thirdly, with an enormous wealth of imagery, that we shall have "glory"; fourthly, that we shall, in some sense, be fed or feasted or entertained; and, finally, that we shall have some sort of official position in the universe—ruling cities, judging angels, being pillars of God's temple. . . . The variation of the promises does not mean that anything other than God will be our ultimate bliss: but because God is more than a Person, and lest we should imagine the joy of His presence too exclusively in terms of our present poor experience of personal love, with all its narrowness and strain and monotony, a dozen changing images, correcting and relieving each other, are supplied. . . . It is written that we shall "stand before" Him, shall appear, shall be inspected. The promise of glory is the promise, almost incredible and only possible by the work of Christ, that some of us, that any of us who really chooses, shall actually survive that examination, shall find approval, shall please God. To please God . . . to be a real ingredient in the divine happiness . . . to be loved by God, not merely pitied, but delighted in as an artist delights in his work or a father in a son—it seems impossible, a weight or burden of glory which our thoughts can hardly sustain. But so it is. . . .

Meanwhile the cross comes before the crown and tomorrow is a Monday morning. A cleft has opened in the pitiless walls of the world, and we are invited to follow our great Captain inside. The following Him is, of course, the essential point.[8]

The phrase "to be a real ingredient in the divine happiness" may need a gloss. It is taken verbatim from Thomas Traherne, a fifteenth-century poet and mystic whose work Lewis often recommended to his correspondents as devotional reading. Traherne's rather daring view is that although we are not *naturally* necessary to God's happiness, by choosing to create us and love us God has to some extent left it up to us whether we shall make God happy by loving Him in return. Thus, though our lack of love cannot make God *un*happy, our free offering of love can make God happy: in that sense we *can* be "a real ingredient in the divine happiness." Strictly speaking, we cannot increase God's happiness, for an infinite amount cannot be increased. But our loving obedience can be one cause of God's happiness: one more mirror by which the divine radiance is reflected back to its source.

In *The Last Battle,* which is the final book of the *Chronicles of Narnia* and one of Lewis's greatest books, the promises Lewis mentions receive fictional embodiment. In Aslan's country at last, the children who are the protagonists of the Narnia stories appear as kings and queens, meet parents and old friends, "And there was greeting and kissing and handshaking and old jokes revived (you've no idea how good an old joke sounds when you take it out again after a rest of five or six hundred years)."[9] Both their physical powers and their senses are raised to new heights: they can swim up waterfalls, see clearly at any distance and run without fatigue. "If one could run without getting tired, I don't think one would want to do anything else." They find that "one can't feel afraid even if one wants to." All of these are images of what Lewis calls a second sense of "glory"—being taken in to nature: "We are summoned to pass in through Nature beyond her into that splendour which she fitfully reflects. And in there beyond Nature we shall eat of the Tree of Life. . . . The faint far-off echoes of those energies which God's creative rapture implanted in matter are what we now call physical pleasures . . . what would it be like to taste at the fountain-head that stream of which even the lower reaches prove so intoxicating. Yet that I believe is what lies before us. The whole man is to drink joy from the fountain of joy."[10]

But the climax of *The Last Battle* is the culminating—almost unbearably poignant—meeting with Aslan:

The light ahead was growing stronger. Lucy saw that a great series of many-colored cliffs led up in front of them like a giant's staircase. And then she forgot everything else, because Aslan himself was coming, leaping down from cliff to cliff like a living cataract of power and beauty. . . . Aslan turned to them and said:

"You do not yet look as happy as I mean you to be."

Lucy said, "We're so afraid of being sent away, Aslan. And you have sent us back into our own world so often."

"No fear of that," said Aslan. "Have you not guessed?"

Their hearts leaped and a wild hope rose within them.

"There *was* a real railway accident," said Aslan softly. "Your father and mother and all of you are—as you call it in the Shadow-Lands— dead. The term is over: the holidays have begun. The dream is ended: this is the morning."

And as He spoke He no longer looked to them like a lion; but the things that began to happen after that were so great and beautiful that I cannot write them. And for us this is the end of all the stories, and we can most truly say that they all lived happily ever after. But for them it was only the beginning of the real story. All their life in this world and all their adventures in Narnia had only been the cover and the title page: now at last they were beginning Chapter One of the Great Story, which no one on earth has read: which goes on for ever: in which every chapter is better than the one before.[11]

Conclusion

"Meanwhile the cross comes before the crown and tomorrow is a Monday morning." What does it all come to, the brilliant dialectic, the splendid rhetoric, the imaginative glory? Has Lewis made a convincing case for Christianity?

If by "convincing" you mean "rationally compelling belief," then the answer is "no." No argument, however conclusive, has the power to *make* us believe. We can always refuse to believe even the strongest evidence: it is this which makes it possible to speak of "deciding" or "choosing" to believe. We cannot, without verging into insanity, manufacture belief with no evidence at all; but we can to some extent pick and choose among the available evidence. Honesty in argument means we must look squarely at all the evidence and give every piece its due weight. That we are compelled to use terms like "due weight" already implies some evaluation: we have to speak of what a "reasonable person," an "impartial judge" would decide on the available evidence.

Well then, would a reasonable person, an impartial judge, be convinced by Lewis's case for the Christian faith? My answer to that is "yes." I count myself a reasonable person, an honest judge of the evidence, and I have been convinced by the arguments given by Lewis, by G. K. Chesterton (who influenced Lewis), and by many other Christian thinkers and writers. I reached this conclusion nearly forty years ago, and none of the reading and thinking I have done since has ever caused me seriously to question that conclusion. I think that I have read and thought about the arguments against Christianity more deeply and sympathetically than those who reject Christianity have read or thought about the case for Christianity.

There are, of course, many honest and intelligent men and women who have sincerely studied the evidence and have rejected Christianity. In many cases, I think that I can see why: they have proceeded from a key misunderstanding of what Christianity really is (as I know it from the inside), a philosophical error that, once made, leads logically to a rejection of Christianity. For instance, one of the most honest and intelligent atheists I know rejected Christianity because he was a "soft determinist": he believed that we can be genuinely free, and at the same time controlled by outside forces. Believing this, he thought that God could have made us free and at the same time caused us always to choose the right. If this were true, then there would be no reason for sin or suffering. Because sin and suffering do exist, he argued that an all-powerful and all-good God could therefore not exist.

Lately, this man has come to question the truth of soft determinism, partly under the influence of an argument like Lewis's "mental proof," which we considered in Chapter 2. He is still a long way from Christianity, but I do not rule out the possibility that he may eventually find his way to it. For reason is given to us by God, and if we follow its golden thread it will lead us back to its Source.

The case for Christianity has convinced me; will it, should it, convince you? If it does, it should not be because of any single book, mine or Lewis's, or any single experience or any single line of argument. As Lewis wrote, "I believe in Christianity as I believe the sun has risen, not only because I see it, but because by it I see everything else."[1] Or, as G. K. Chesterton wrote, "[A man] is partially convinced when he has found this or that proof for a thing and he can expound it. But a man is not really convinced of a philosophical theory when he finds that something proves it. He is only really convinced when he finds that everything proves it. And the more converging reasons he finds pointing to this conviction the more bewildered he is if asked suddenly to sum them up. . . . That very multiplicity of proof which ought to make reply overwhelming makes reply impossible."[2]

But, of course, what we cannot "suddenly sum up," we can sum up given time and sympathetic attention; the case for Christianity can be made. And of those who have made it in our generation, C. S. Lewis has, I think, done it best, partly because his wide-ranging genius has enabled him to give so many of the "converging reasons," to appeal to our intellect as well as our imagination, to literature and history as well as logic.

I began this book by exploring some general reasons for Lewis's success; in the course of the book I hope that I have filled in those generalities and made them concrete. If nothing else, I hope I have sent you to Lewis himself, or back to Lewis himself, to examine his arguments in their context and to study *in extenso* what I have been forced to summarize or briefly quote. And, of course, Lewis himself wants you to look beyond him, to his Master, Christ, and to the many great writers who have made the case for the Christian faith for their own time and for all times. It matters very little whether Lewis, or I, win or lose any particular argument, are seen as victor or defeated. It matters a great deal that you, the reader, should know the truth, and that the truth should make you free.

Notes

Chapter 1

1. *Time*, 5 December 1977, p. 92.
2. *Time*, 7 April 1980, p. 66.
3. Lewis to Miss Rhona Bodle, 11 March 1945.*
4. C. S. Lewis, *God in the Dock* (Grand Rapids, Mich: Wm. B. Eerdmans Publishing Co., 1970), p. 96.
5. Ibid., p. 183.
6. Ibid., p. 179.
7. C. S. Lewis, *Surprised by Joy* (New York: Harcourt Brace Jovanovich, 1955), p. 115.
8. C. S. Lewis, *An Experiment in Criticism* (Cambridge: Cambridge University Press, 1961), pp. 85–86.
9. C. S. Lewis, *The World's Last Night and Other Essays* (New York: Harcourt Brace Jovanovich, 1960), p. 17.
10. Lewis to Arthur Greeves, 12 September 1933, in *They Stand Together*, ed. Walter Hooper (New York: Macmillan Publishing Co., 1979), pp. 462–465.
11. C. S. Lewis, *The Silver Chair* (New York: Macmillan Publishing Co., Collier Books, 1956), pp. 155–156.
12. C. S. Lewis, *The Weight of Glory and Other Addresses* (New York: Macmillan Publishing Co., 1980), p. 60.
13. Ibid., pp. 68–69.
14. Lewis to Miss Rhona Bodle, 11 March 1945.*
15. Lewis to Sister Madelva, 19 March 1963.*
16. Lewis to Ruth Pittinger, 17 July 1951.*

Chapter 2

1. Lewis to Warren Lewis, 24 October 1931, in *Letters of C. S. Lewis*, ed. W. H. Lewis (New York: Harcourt Brace Jovanovich, 1966), pp. 143–144.
2. C. S. Lewis, *The Silver Chair* (New York: Macmillan Publishing Co., Collier Books, 1956), p. 159.
3. Lewis to Miss Jacob, 3 July 1941.*

*Originals of previously unpublished letters (asterisked throughout the notes) are in the Bodleian Library, Oxford, or in the Marion E. Wade Collection, Wheaton College, Wheaton, Illinois.

4. Lewis to Dom Bede Griffiths, 28 May 1952, in *Letters of C. S. Lewis*, ed. W. H. Lewis, p. 242.
5. Lewis to Dom Bede Griffiths, 7 January 1936.*
6. C. S. Lewis, *Letters to Malcolm: Chiefly on Prayer* (New York: Harcourt Brace Jovanovich, 1955), pp. 63–65.
7. C. S. Lewis, *That Hideous Strength* (New York: Macmillan Publishing Co., 1946), pp. 301–308).
8. *Time*, 7 April 1980, p. 66.
9. A clear and balanced account of this encounter may be found in Walter Hooper, "Oxford's Bonnie Fighter," in *C. S. Lewis at the Breakfast Table*, ed. James T. Como (New York: Macmillan Publishing Co., 1979), pp. 161–165.
10. C. S. Lewis, *Miracles, A Preliminary Study* (New York: Macmillan Publishing Co., 1947), pp. 22–23.
11. C. S. Lewis, *Miracles*, rev. ed. (New York: Macmillan Publishing Co., 1960), p. 22.

Chapter 3

1. C. S. Lewis, *The Screwtape Letters* (New York: Macmillan Publishing Co., 1942), p. 33.
2. C. S. Lewis, *Letters to Malcolm: Chiefly on Prayer* (New York: Harcourt Brace Jovanovich, 1955), pp. 21–22.
3. See C. S. Lewis, *Mere Christianity* (New York: Macmillan Publishing Co., 1960), pp. 145–149; and Lewis, *Screwtape*, pp. 127–129.
4. Lewis, *Letters to Malcolm*, pp. 51, 52.
5. C. S. Lewis, *The Problem of Pain* (New York: Macmillan Publishing Co., 1940), pp. 83–85.
6. Lewis to Sister Penelope, 30 December 1950.*
7. Lewis to a Lady, 12 September 1951, in *Letters of C. S. Lewis*, ed. W. H. Lewis (New York: Harcourt Brace Jovanovich, 1966), p. 234.
8. Lewis to Miss Jacob, 15 August 1941.*
9. Lewis to a Lady, 28 November 1950, in W. H. Lewis, *Letters*, p. 233.
10. Lewis, *Pain*, pp. 106–107.
11. C. S. Lewis, *The Great Divorce* (New York: Macmillan Publishing Co., 1946), pp. 120–121.
12. Lewis, *Letters to Malcolm*, p. 90.
13. Lewis, *Mere Christianity*, p. 141.
14. Ibid., p. 153.

Chapter 4

1. C. S. Lewis, *Mere Christianity* (New York: Macmillan Publishing Co., 1960), p. 56.
2. C. S. Lewis, *God in the Dock* (Grand Rapids, Mich.: Wm. B. Eerdmans Publishing Co., 1970), p. 180.
3. Ibid., p. 157.

4. Lewis to Arthur Greeves, 11 December 1944, in *They Stand Together*, ed. Walter Hooper (New York: Macmillan Publishing Co, 1979), p. 503.
5. Lewis, *God in the Dock*, pp. 157–158.
6. Ibid., p. 159.
7. Lewis, *Mere Christianity*, p. 57.
8. C. S. Lewis, *The Lion, The Witch and the Wardrobe* (New York: Macmillan Publishing Co., Collier Books, 1950), p. 140.
9. Lewis, *Mere Christianity*, p. 60.
10. Nevill Coghill, "An Approach to English," in *Light on C. S. Lewis*, ed. Jocelyn Gibb (New York: Harcourt Brace Jovanovich, 1965), p. 63.
11. Lewis to Sister Penelope CSMV, 6 November 1957, in *Letters of C. S. Lewis*, ed. W. H. Lewis (New York: Harcourt Brace Jovanovich, 1966), p. 280.
12. C. S. Lewis, "Modern Theology and Biblical Criticism," in *Christian Reflections*, ed. Walter Hooper (Grand Rapids, Mich.: Wm. B. Eerdmans Publishing Co., 1967), pp. 153–154, 157–158.
13. G. K. Chesterton, *The Everlasting Man* (Garden City, N.J.: Doubleday and Company, 1955), p. 208.

Chapter 5

1. Letter to Mr. Canfield, 28 February 1955.*
2. C. S. Lewis, *Reflections on the Psalms* (New York: Harcourt Brace Jovanovich, 1958), pp. 109–110.
3. C. S. Lewis, *Miracles*, rev. ed. (New York: Macmillan Publishing Co., 1960), pp. 101–102.
4. Ibid., p. 106.
5. Ibid., p. 167–168.
6. Ibid., p. 132–133.
7. Ibid., p. 133.
8. Ibid., p. 139.

Chapter 6

1. C. S. Lewis, *The World's Last Night and Other Essays* (New York: Harcourt Brace Jovanovich, 1960), p. 17.
2. Ibid., pp. 15–16.
3. Ibid., p. 15.
4. Ibid., pp. 25–26, 29–30.
5. C. S. Lewis, *Perelandra* (New York; Macmillan Publishing Co., 1965), p. 13.
6. C. S. Lewis, *Mere Christianity* (New York: Macmillan Publishing Co., 1960), pp. 123–124.
7. C. S. Lewis, *The Screwtape Letters.* (New York: Macmillan Publishing Co., 1942), p. 38.
8. C. S. Lewis, *God in the Dock* (Grand Rapids, Mich: Wm. B. Eerdmans Publishing Co., 1970), p. 173.

Chapter 7

1. Lewis to Dom Bede Griffiths, undated, 1930.*
2. Lewis to Dom Bede Griffiths, 27 June 1949.*
3. C. S. Lewis, *The Last Battle* (New York: Macmillan Publishing Co., Collier Books, 1956), pp. 164–165.
4. Lewis to a Lady, 8 November 1952, in *Letters of C. S. Lewis*, ed. W. H. Lewis (New York: Harcourt Brace Jovanovich, 1966), p. 247.
5. Lewis to Dom Bede Griffiths, 27 September 1948.*
6. C. S. Lewis, *God in the Dock* (Grand Rapids, Mich: Wm. B. Eerdmans Publishing Co., 1970), pp. 102–103.
7. C. S. Lewis, *Till We Have Faces* (New York: Harcourt Brace Jovanovich, 1956), p. 295.
8. C. S. Lewis, *The Weight of Glory and Other Addresses* (New York: Macmillan Publishing Co., 1980), pp. 79–80.
9. Lewis to Dom Bede Griffiths, June 1937.*
10. C. S. Lewis, *Out of the Silent Planet* (New York: Macmillan Publishing Co., 1965), pp. 136–137.
11. *Destinies* 1, no. 3 (1979).
12. Lewis, *God in the Dock*, pp. 320–321.
13. C. S. Lewis, *Of Other Worlds* (New York: Harcourt Brace Jovanovich, 1966), p. 84.
14. Lewis, *The Weight of Glory*, pp. 91–92.

Chapter 8

1. C. S. Lewis, *Reflections on the Psalms* (New York: Harcourt Brace Jovanovich, 1958), p. 7.
2. Ibid., p. 61.
3. C. S. Lewis, *Mere Christianity* (New York: Macmillan Publishing Co., 1960), pp. 86–87.
4. C. S. Lewis, "The Poison of Subjectivism," in *Christian Reflections*, ed. Walter Hooper (Grand Rapids, Mich: Wm. B. Eerdmans Publishing Co., 1967), pp. 53–54.
5. Lewis to Mr. Masson, 6 March 1956.*
6. C. S. Lewis, *God in the Dock* (Grand Rapids, Mich: Wm B. Eerdmans Publishing Co., 1970), p. 320.
7. Lewis to Miss Rhona Bodle, 28 April 1955.*
8. Lewis, *God in the Dock*, p. 273.
9. C. S. Lewis, The Screwtape Letters, (New York: Macmillan Publishing Co., 1942), pp. 101–102.
10. Lewis to Dom Bede Griffiths, 24 December 1946.*
11. W. H. Lewis, *Letters of C. S. Lewis* (New York: Harcourt Brace Jovanovich, 1966), p. 21.
12. C. S. Lewis, *The World's Last Night and Other Essays* (New York: Harcourt Brace Jovanovich, 1960), p. 75.

13. C. S. Lewis, *The Weight of Glory and Other Addresses* (New York: Macmillan Publishing Co., 1980), pp. 21–22, 25.

14. Cf. Chapter 4, "The sort of thing a man might say," in *The Inklings*, Humphrey Carpenter (Boston: Houghton Mifflin Co., 1979).

Chapter 9

1. C. S. Lewis, *The World's Last Night and Other Essays* (New York: Harcourt Brace Jovanovich, 1960), pp. 5–6.

2. C. S. Lewis, *The Screwtape Letters* (New York: Macmillan Publishing Co., 1942), pp. 127–128.

3. Lewis, *The World's Last Night*, p. 9.

4. Ibid., p. 8.

5. Lewis, *Screwtape*, pp. 26–27.

6. Lewis to a Lady, 15 May 1952, in *Letters of C. S. Lewis*, ed. W. H. Lewis (New York: Harcourt Brace Jovanovich, 1966), p. 241.

7. C. S. Lewis, "Petitionary Prayer," in *Christian Reflections*, ed. Walter Hooper (Grand Rapids, Mich· Wm B Eerdmans Publishing Co., 1967), p. 149.

8. C. S. Lewis, *Letters to Malcolm: Chiefly on Prayer* (New York: Harcourt Brace Jovanovich, 1955), p. 60.

9. Ibid., pp. 85, 86.

10. Ibid., pp. 65–66.

11. Lewis, *Screwtape*, p. 17.

12. C. S. Lewis, *Reflections on the Psalms* (New York: Harcourt Brace Jovanovich, 1958), pp. 94–97.

13. Ibid., pp. 1–2.

Chapter 10

1. C. S. Lewis, *English Literature in the 16th Century*, vol. 2 (Oxford: Oxford University Press, 1954), p. 187.

2. C. S. Lewis, *God in the Dock* (Grand Rapids, Mich.: Wm. B. Eerdmans Publishing Co., 1970), pp. 130–131.

3. C. S. Lewis, *The Problem of Pain* (New York: Macmillan Publishing Co., 1940), p. 133.

4. C. S. Lewis, *Reflections on the Psalms* (New York: Harcourt Brace Jovanovich, 1958), pp. 40–42.

5. C. S. Lewis, *Letters to Malcolm: Chiefly on Prayer* (New York: Harcourt Brace Jovanovich, 1955), pp. 121–124.

6. C. S. Lewis, *The Allegory of Love* (Oxford: Oxford University Press, 1936), p. 155.

7. C. S. Lewis, *The Silver Chair* (New York: Macmillan Publishing Co., Collier Books, 1956), pp. 10–11.

8. C. S. Lewis, *The Weight of Glory and Other Addresses* (New York: Macmillan Publishing Co., 1980), pp. 10–11, 13, 18–19.

9. C. S. Lewis, *The Last Battle* (New York: Macmillan Publishing Co., Collier Books, 1956), p. 179.
10. Lewis, *The Weight of Glory*, p. 18.
11. Lewis, *The Last Battle*, pp. 182–184.

Conclusion

1. C. S. Lewis, *The Weight of Glory and Other Addresses* (New York: Macmillan Publishing Co., 1980), p. 92.
2. G. K. Chesterton, *Orthodoxy* (Garden City, N.J.: Doubleday and Company, 1959), p. 83.

Suggested Further Readings

About forty of C. S. Lewis's books are still in print, but some of his more scholarly or specialized books are not of interest to the general reader. What follows is a list of all the books by Lewis that are likely to be of interest to the nonspecialist reader. Each book's original publication date in England is followed by bibliographic data for American editions. I have added to this list a handful of the best recent studies of Lewis. (Unfortunately, some excellent older studies of Lewis are now out of print; these are marked with an asterisk.) Almost all of the books on this list can be obtained in paperback; the out-of-print books can be found in most good libraries.

Books by C. S. Lewis

The Abolition of Man: Reflections on Education with Special Reference to the Teaching of English in the Upper Forms of Schools. 1943. New York: Macmillan, 1947; paperback, 1965.

Christian Reflections. Edited by Walter Hooper. Grand Rapids: W. B. Eerdmans, 1967.

The Dark Tower and Other Stories. Edited and with a Preface by Walter Hooper. 1977. New York: Harcourt Brace Jovanovich, 1977; paperback, 1977.

The Four Loves. 1960. New York: Harcourt Brace Jovanovich, 1960; paperback, 1971.

God in the Dock: Essays in Theology and Ethics. Edited and with a Preface by Walter Hooper. 1970 (originally published as *Undeceptions*). Grand Rapids: W. B. Eerdmans, 1970.

The Great Divorce. 1945. New York: Macmillan, 1946; paperback, 1963.

A Grief Observed. 1961 (published under the pseudonym N. W. Clerk). New York: Seabury, 1963 (published under the pseudonym N. W. Clerk); New York: Bantam Books, 1976 (paperback; published under the name C. S. Lewis, with an Afterword by Chad Walsh).

The Horse and His Boy. Illustrated by Pauline Baynes. 1954. New York: Macmillan, 1954; paperback, 1970.

The Last Battle. Illustrated by Pauline Baynes. 1956. New York: Macmillan, 1956; paperback, 1970.

Letters of C. S. Lewis. Edited and with a Memoir by W. H. Lewis. 1975. New York: Harcourt Brace Jovanovich, 1975; paperback, 1975.

Letters to an American Lady. Edited by Clyde Kilby. Grand Rapids: W. B. Eerdmans, 1967; New York: Pyramid, 1971 (paperback).

Letters to Malcolm: Chiefly on Prayer. 1964. New York: Harcourt Brace Jovanovich, 1964; paperback, 1973.

The Lion, the Witch and the Wardrobe. Illustrated by Pauline Baynes. 1950. New York: Macmillan, 1950; paperback, 1970.

The Magician's Nephew. Illustrated by Pauline Baynes. London: 1955. New York: Macmillan, 1955; paperback, 1970.

Mere Christianity. A revised and enlarged edition, with a new introduction, of three books, *The Case for Christianity* (in England, *Broadcast Talks*), 1942; *Christian Behavior,* 1943; and *Beyond Personality,* 1944. 1952. New York: Macmillan, 1952; paperback, 1960.

Miracles: A Preliminary Study. 1947. New York: Macmillan, 1947; paperback, 1963.

Of Other Worlds: Essays and Stories. Edited and with a Preface by Walter Hooper. New York: Harcourt Brace Jovanovich, 1966; paperback, 1975.

Out of the Silent Planet. 1938. New York: Macmillan, 1943; paperback, 1965.

Perelandra. 1943. New York: Macmillan, 1944; paperback, 1965.

The Pilgrim's Regress: An Allegorical Apology for Christianity, Reason, and Romanticism. 1933. New York: Sheed and Ward, 1935. With the author's important new Preface on Romanticism, as well as added footnotes, and running head explaining the allegory, 1943. New York: Sheed and Ward, 1944; Grand Rapids: W. B. Eerdmans, 1958.

Prince Caspian. Illustrated by Pauline Baynes. 1951. New York: Macmillan, 1951; paperback, 1970.

The Problem of Pain. 1940. New York: Macmillan, 1943, 1977; paperback, 1962.

Reflections on the Psalms. 1958. New York: Harcourt Brace Jovanovich, 1958; paperback, 1964.

The Screwtape Letters. 1942. New York: Macmillan, 1943; paperback, 1959.

The Silver Chair. Illustrated by Pauline Baynes. 1953. New York: Macmillan, 1953; paperback, 1970.

Surprised by Joy: The Shape of My Early Life. 1955. New York: Harcourt
Brace Jovanovich, 1956; paperback, 1966.
That Hideous Strength. 1945. New York: Macmillan, 1946; paperback,
1965.
Till We Have Faces: A Myth Retold. 1956. New York: Harcourt Brace
Jovanovich, 1957; Grand Rapids: W. B. Eerdmans, 1966
(paperback).
The Voyage of the "Dawn Treader." Illustrated by Pauline Baynes. 1952.
New York: Macmillan, 1952; paperback, 1970.
The Weight of Glory and Other Addresses. 1949 (originally published as
Transposition and Other Addresses). New York: Macmillan, 1949;
Grand Rapids: W. B. Eerdmans, 1965.
The World's Last Night and Other Essays. New York: Harcourt Brace
Jovanovich, 1960; paperback, 1973.

Books About C. S. Lewis

Carpenter, Humphrey. *The Inklings.* London: Allen & Unwin, 1978.
Christopher, Joe R., and Ostling, Joan K. *C. S. Lewis: An Annotated
Checklist of Writings About Him and His Works.* Kent, Ohio: Kent
State University Press, 1974.
Como, James, ed. *"C. S. Lewis at the Breakfast Table" and Other
Recollections.* New York: Macmillan, 1979.
*Cunningham, Richard B. *C. S. Lewis: Defender of the Faith.*
Philadelphia: Westminster Press, 1967.
Gibb, Joselyn, ed. *Light on C. S. Lewis.* (Essays by Owen Barfield,
Austin Farrar, J. A. W. Bennett, Nevill Coghill, John Lawlor,
Stella Gibbons, Kathleen Raine, Chad Walsh, and Walter
Hooper.) 1965. New York: Harcourt, Brace & World, 1965;
paperback, 1976
Gibson, Evan. *C. S. Lewis, Spinner of Tales.* Grand Rapids: W. B.
Eerdmans, 1980.
Green, Roger Lancelyn, and Hooper, Walter. *C. S. Lewis: A Biography.*
1974. New York: Harcourt Brace Jovanovich, 1974; paperback,
1976.
Howard, Thomas. *The Achievement of C. S. Lewis.* Wheaton, Ill.: Harold
Shaw, 1980.
Kilby, Clyde S. *The Christian World of C. S. Lewis.* Grand Rapids: W. B.
Eerdmans, 1964.
———. *Images of Salvation in the Fiction of C. S. Lewis.* Wheaton, Ill.:
Harold Shaw, 1978.
*Kreeft, Peter. *C. S. Lewis: A Critical Essay.* Grand Rapids: W. B.
Eerdmans, 1969 (paperback).

*Purtill, Richard. *Lord of the Elves and Eldils: Fantasy and Philosophy in C. S. Lewis and J. R. R. Tolkien.* Grand Rapids: Zondervan, 1974 (paperback).

Schakel, Peter, Jr., ed. *The Longing for a Form: Essays on the Fiction of C. S. Lewis.* Kent, Ohio: Kent State University Press, 1977.

Vanauken, Sheldon. *A Severe Mercy.* 1977. San Francisco: Harper & Row, 1977.

*Walsh, Chad. *C. S. Lewis: Apostle to the Skeptics.* New York: Macmillan, 1949; Folcraft, Pa: Folcraft Library Editions, 1974.

Walsh, Chad, *The Literary Legacy of C. S. Lewis.* New York: Harcourt Brace Jovanovich, 1980.

Index